*Business Process Management,*
*Basics and Beyond*

# HOW

# WORK

## GETS DONE

## first edition

*Business Process Management, Basics and Beyond*

# HOW

# WORK

## GETS DONE

first edition

# Arjit Singh Mahal

# Technics Publications

New Jersey

Published by:

**Technics Publications, LLC**
Post Office Box 161
Bradley Beach, NJ 07720 U.S.A.
www.technicspub.com

Edited by Carol Lehn
Cover design by Mark Brye
Diagrams by Mike Foresman

| ISBN, print ed. | 978-1-9355040-7-8 |
| ISBN, ePub ed. | 978-1-9355043-5-1 |
| ISBN, Kindle ed. | 978-1-9355043-6-8 |

First Printing 2010
Library of Congress Control Number: 2010932820

ATTENTION SCHOOLS AND BUSINESSES: Technics Publications books are available at quantity discounts with bulk purchase for educational, business, or sales promotional use. For information, please write to Technics Publications, PO Box 161, Bradley Beach, NJ 07090, or email Steve Hoberman, President of Technics Publications, at me@stevehoberman.com.

*This is a practitioner's story. The book captures the voice of over 3 decades of Mr. Mahal's experience of how work gets done, and how to do it better in the global economy driven by the unrelenting pressures of change and opportunity. I will not hesitate to recommend this book to executives and operational managers responsible for orchestrating 21st century organizations and supply chains.*

Amit Mitra
Senior Manager
Tata Consultancy Services America

*Arjit Mahal's new book on Business Process Management (BPM),* **How Work Gets Done**, *is a timely and highly readable introduction to the integrative role of business processes in any organization. I recommend the book to business managers who are seeking to add value, regardless of their functional specialization.*

Sharan Jagpal
Professor
Rutgers Business School

**How Work Gets Done** *is a clear, concise, and well-navigated journey into the world of Business Processes and Business Process Management. From a practical introduction through to advanced topics around methodology and competencies, it is suitable for business process newcomers and seasoned practitioners, alike. It should be required reading at all levels of every organization.*

Eugene Fucetola
Operations Manager
Global Application Messaging and Integration
Mars Information Services

*Arjit Mahal is one of the most knowledgeable and gifted instructors I have known. Before he began teaching others about business process management, he had served as head of the BPM initiative at Mars Americas in implementing business process practice. He brings all that knowledge and all the practical insights he has acquired consulting with a wide variety of other organizations to this wonderful introduction to business process change. If you've always wished you had a very practical friend who could sit down and talk you through just what's involved in improving how work gets done at your organization, this is the book!*

Paul Harmon
Executive Editor, Business Process Trends
Chief Methodologist, BPTrends Associates

*Artie Mahal has done something that was thought to be impossible – produce an easily readable book about business process management. He paints pictures with words, offers many easy-to-grasp analogies, and stimulates with simplifying charts of complex concepts. The book captures a wide audience, including the student with limited business experience, the business manager seeking practical skills, and the employee who is just curious about the business world.*

Leon Fraser
Lecturer
Rutgers Business School


***How Work Gets Done** provides a very structured approach to both describing and understanding businesses processes. It is a must read for any enterprise architect or processes analyst striving to add value to their organization.*

Edward M L Peters
CEO
OpenConnect
Author of **The Paid for Option**

# Contents at a Glance

# Contents

*To Dr. Jasjit Balwant Atwal and*

*Dr. Manmohan Singh Atwal*

*Thanks for the break!*

# Acknowledgements

My journey into the business process profession would not have started without the opportunity given to me by the late Steve Kienitz, President of Information Services International (now Mars Information Services). He gave me the role of implementing business and process change into Mars' North American business units. I needed an expert in business process management to help me in the successful implementation of this program. I was fortunate to have Roger Burlton help me roll out this program and he became my coach and mentor, and thus my Process Guru.

Upon my retirement from Mars, Incorporated, in addition to starting my own consulting business, I joined BPTrends Associates as a senior consultant. My association with Paul Harmon gave me an opportunity to work with and learn from this accomplished business process methodologist. I also thank Celia Wolf for giving me the opportunity to teach and practice Business Process Management— which helped me further shape my thoughts for writing this book.

My many thanks to several process professional colleagues from whom, over the years, I have picked up ideas through discussions and debates while working in the business process discipline. These include Beth Beasley, Michael Chyzowych, Sandra Foster, Kathy Long, Mary Lowe, Alexandre Magno Mello, Amit Mitra, Gregory Paul, Laura Reed, Richard Simourd, Brent Sabean, and Roger Tregear.

Thanks very much to Kiran Garimella for encouraging me to write this book and giving useful tips along the way. Vincent Arrechi and Eugene Fucetola were instrumental in helping me develop the BPM competencies matrix, and Robert Bandel in validating the process configuration model usage for analysis. Sandra Foster helped in thinking through the process modeling guide and Roger Burlton provided valuable insights in the foundational concepts.

This book would not have been possible without the dedicated help of my colleague, Mike Foresman, in developing numerous diagrams. His challenging questions helped shape the diagrams for effective communication. I am indebted to him for his effort.

My publisher, Steve Hoberman, is a former colleague and, since then, a good friend. I am grateful to him for offering to publish this book through his publishing organization—making it easier to go through the process. Steve put me in touch with a uniquely qualified editor for this book, Carol Lehn. Carol was excellent in editing the book. She found inconsistencies in the details of the topics, which made me think even harder to ensure the validity of my statements.

Last, but not least, thanks to my daughter, Apara Mahal, for reviewing the book, and to my wife, Millie Mahal, for letting me defer actions on her to-do list while I was engaged in writing.

I like Artie's new book, ***How Work Gets Done***! It is clear. It is concise. It gets to the point. You don't have to be a programmer or a mathematician to understand it. He uses good old, plain, everyday words, not some arcane technical or modeling language. You can read it, get the point, and start getting right to work. How much better could it get?

Having said all of that, it is my perception that this is not a book for technicians, either computer technicians or business process modeling technicians. This is a book for people who need to understand the issues and make something happen. I am not saying that a technical audience would not benefit from the book...quite the contrary. There is ample material and examples for producing diagrammatic representations of business processes. There is a lot of material on skills and responsibilities and on managing business process management projects. Artie obviously has had a lot of experience doing business process work and getting the concepts ingrained at times, in somewhat reluctant environments. The book has a lot of technical as well as managerial wisdom.

However, I am sure that Artie will come under some degree of criticism from the Business Process aficionados. For example, in one popular graphic notation standard in the Business Process domain, I understand there are 16 different icons to represent 16 different kinds of events that can be modeled. Good night! I am not too sure that even I want to know that much about it. That would be information overload for me. I am also sure that there comes a time in every Business Process experience when that kind of event differentiation becomes a significant issue (and Artie's book does not preclude that in any way); but this book is elegant in its focus on the Business, not the Systems. He leaves you with the distinct impression, "we need to get started working on this!" He is not intimidating you with the excruciating detail that may necessarily come later.

Artie says at one point, "I remember an incident where a senior IT executive, upon being advised to define business processes before developing systems, made this statement: 'We are in the business of developing systems, what do we have to do with processes?'" My point in the above sentence is, Business Processes are not about writing code, they are about managing the Business. There comes a time when writing code is important, but the fundamental issue is managing the Business.

By the way, until we understand something about the Business Processes, I would observe that it is little wonder that for the last 15 or 20 years or more, "Alignment" has been in the top 10 issues (if not the top issue) in the CEO surveys that management says IT must address. Until you understand something about the Business Processes, I would suggest that there is little probability that the code you write will have anything to do with management's perception of the Business! "Alignment" *is* the problem, and until you define what you're aligning to, there is little probability of producing anything that is what I would call "vertically" aligned.

Artie also makes the point that the data has to be aligned with the processes (which I would call "horizontally" aligned). I would make the additional observation that if you cannot definitively associate the inputs and outputs of the processes with some attributes of the entities in your data model (when you get around to building the systems), all of the information in your Enterprise is transient data. You will be spending substantial amounts of General and Administrative Expenses trying to reconcile misunderstandings and trying to find (and manage) the "real" data.

I have spent most of my professional life trying to understand Enterprise Architecture and Artie has given us a clear and concise statement of one of the critical aspects of the Enterprise, Business Process Management. I wish I had as clear and concise a statement of Inventory Management (from which the data derives), of Distribution Management (the basis for the Networks), of Organization (responsibility) Management, of Timing Management and of Motivation Management. It would complete my library. Maybe I can enlist Artie to start working on several more books!

Artie...thank you for your good Business Process work on *How Work Gets Done*.

John A. Zachman
President, Zachman International

This book content is meant for a broad audience that ranges from process people management to business and process analysts, technical analysts, and even college students preparing to enter the workforce. As the sub-title of this book suggests, "Basics and Beyond": Chapters 1 to 7 outline the basic foundation of processes in an organization and are meant for all readers—irrespective of their professional area of engagement; whereas Chapters 8 to 12 are more geared towards process owners/managers, process practitioners including business analysts, performance analysts, and technology analysts. Overall, there are valuable takeaways for everyone in the workforce. The following outline briefly describes each chapter's content:

- **Chapter 1 Enterprise Business Model.** This chapter introduces the basic structure of a generic organization, showing how all parts of an organization function in an integrated and unified way. The organization may be viewed conceptually in two parts: planning and operations. The business processes take inputs from the suppliers and transform them into products and services for the customers. The people, technology, and supporting infrastructure serve as the enablers in this transformation. While these enablers are traditionally considered an asset, business processes must be viewed as a "super asset" without which the enabling assets would have little value. This point of view establishes the basic reason for business process management.

- **Chapter 2 Business Process Hierarchy.** Business processes have an inherent hierarchy describing how work gets done from a higher to a lower-level of detail. These hierarchy levels are an abstract way of understanding and managing the enterprise. This chapter introduces the basic structure and purpose of hierarchy levels. For example, Levels 1 and 2 are considered to be the *Process Architecture* or *Blueprint* of an organization, and are used for setting strategic intent; Whereas Level 3 and below describe transactional work where the "rubber meets the road", so to say. When process Levels 3 and below are automated, they become transactional systems. Therefore, for any automation of work, the process must be defined first.

- **Chapter 3 Business Process Blueprint.** An organization may have hundreds of business processes at various levels of detail. To effectively use them, there needs to be a methodical approach for understanding and utilizing them. This chapter introduces a proven format for organizing the enterprise processes into Process Architecture or a Blueprint. This Blueprint is driven by the organizational mission, vision, and strategies to provide competitive advantage through effective governance of process assets. This Blueprint and the philosophy of process management, when integrated into the culture of an organization, enable effective change and transformation.

- **Chapter 4 Anatomy of a Process.** A process may be simply defined as "how work gets done". Every process has a common "anatomy", a structure: inputs, outputs, guides and enablers. Triggered by an event, a process receives inputs from suppliers or other processes and then transforms them into outputs and outcomes. The inputs generally are material, data, and states of things. The guides provide the controls and knowledge, and the enablers provide people, technology, and infrastructure. Data is used in all areas: inputs, outputs, guides, enablers, and even trigger events. The understanding of a process "anatomy" provides the basis for managing all parts that make up the whole process.

- **Chapter 5 Process Knowledge.** Business processes are an organizational asset. The information about them must be documented, preserved, and shared across the organization for reuse. The process information can be in multiple formats, such as text and diagrams, and also at various levels of detail, depending upon their level in the hierarchy. An organization must establish a minimum standard for documenting and making them available for use by its employees. This chapter is a basic guide for managing process knowledge assets.

- **Chapter 6 Business Models.** Models, or "Maps", are a visual representation of patterns and their meaning that facilitate understanding and communication about topics of interest. They simplify complexity by using diagrams, pictures, scenarios, simulation patterns, and icons that are relevant to the subject at hand for the intended audience. This chapter outlines process and data modeling practices and standards that may be used by process performers, managers, and analysts to define how their work gets done. While IT analysts and technicians should understand this language to effectively translate it into technical specifications, technical models are out of the scope of this book.

- **Chapter 7 Process Configuration.** Enterprise performance is delivered through the execution of one or more business processes in an organization. Business processes have two sets of elements that support execution: The guide elements, which are Organization and Strategies, Stakeholder Relationships, and Policies and Rules; and enable elements, which are Human Capital, Enabling Technology, and Supporting Infrastructure. Information is used and Knowledge is created throughout all of these elements via relevant Business Processes. Business Processes and their guides and enablers are critical assets of an organization. They must be understood, aligned, and optimized to ensure delivery of desired and sustainable performance. This chapter introduces the *Process Configuration Model,* which is a practical tool for understanding and synchronizing all elements for effectiveness and efficiency.

- **Chapter 8 BPM Methodology.** There are many methodologies that analyze processes in the current state and propose a future state of transformation. These are primarily at the process-level of change, while providing some or little enterprise-level context. A methodology which considers all parts of process change throughout the enterprise is essential. BPTrends Associates' *BPM Methodology* is just such a comprehensive framework. It constitutes three integrated tiers of business process management and change at the Enterprise Level, Process Level, and Implementation Level.

This chapter provides a step-by-step introduction of this proven methodology.

- **Chapter 9 BPM Competencies.** Business process improvement is a collaborative effort among several professional practices, supported by specialists who contribute a variety of skills. The professional practices include *Strategic Planning, Program and Project Management, Business Process Management (BPM), Organization Development & Design (OD),* and Technologies, including *Information Technology (IT).* The job titles of individuals in these roles vary across organizations. This chapter describes the competencies required for various roles that support business process and allied disciplines.

- **Chapter 10 BPM Services.** To support the professional practice of Business Process Management (BPM), an organization should have a go-to organizational entity where workers, managers, management, analysts, and project teams can seek advice, training, coaching, and other assistance in the application of methods and tools for improving processes. Many organizations establish a go-to organization unit for Information Technology (IT) as their BPM discipline evolves. IT plays a custodial role because process discipline helps their mission of developing applications. This chapter provides a step-by-step method for creating a *Center of Excellence* to support BPM services.

- **Chapter 11 Software Tools.** There are two broad areas of process-enabling tools and technology. Business processes are enabled by application systems software for individual or enterprise-wide applications such as *ERP (Enterprise Resource Planning),* and there are also software tools that enable the analysis, design, automation, and monitoring of business processes. The first area of business software is out of scope for this book, but a brief outline is provided on the type of current tool sets used by business process practitioners in this continually changing marketplace.

- **Chapter 12 NewAge Foods Business Process Case Study.** NewAge Foods is a fictitious organization. This is a hypothetical case study of its **Recruit and Hire Employees** process which has several performance issues. This chapter utilizes the process-level methodology steps discussed in Chapter 8 and introduces a simplified, yet proven checklist of steps to be undertaken for the scoping, analysis, and improvement of a process. The purpose of this chapter is to show, by example, some of the key deliverable samples, techniques, and templates that can be used by the reader with ease.

## Case Study: The NewAge Foods Company

To describe basic concepts, techniques, and methods of business process know how, I have chosen a fictitious business called NewAge Foods Company. My intent is to create business process understanding using simple examples, but not to necessarily solve business problems using a specific case study. Also, in Chapter 12, where a business process change example is used, my objective is to show, by example, the steps and some sample key deliverables and templates of the Business Process Management (BPM) methodology used in this book. The intent is not to provide all details, as this is not a tutorial for the methodology.

The following is a brief introduction to this business, the elements of which are conceptually similar to an organization engaged in the manufacturing and selling of food products. The examples used in this book will be based on this NewAge Foods Company.

The NewAge Foods Company makes foods containing antioxidants and other supplements consistent with popular trends in the marketplace. The business is a family-owned operation based on the East Coast of the United States. The company primarily focuses on ready-to-eat snacks, which are sold through various channels that include grocery stores, pharmacies, theaters, health stores, and vending outlets. In addition to the mass production of snacks, such as cookies and energy bars, the company produces specialized snacks such as cookies for diabetics—which they sell through their mail-order part of the business.

NewAge develops product ideas, markets, sells, manufactures, and ships all of their wholesale products to customers through a broker. But they sell customized products directly to consumers through an e-mail/mail-order process. The organization is structured around traditional functions such as Finance, Research & Development, Marketing, Sales, Procurement, Manufacturing, and Logistics. The supporting functions include Human Resources, Information Technology, and Facilities Management.

In today's fast-paced, continually changing business environment, whether the world is flat or curved and work is outsourced or insourced, the basic nature of how work gets done and who does the work, is still fundamental to personal effectiveness and organizational productivity for creating value in terms of products and services.

Business is an interaction between processes, people, and technology, supported by an underlying infrastructure. Business processes are how work gets done, people are who do the work, and technology is how we enable the work, the underlying mechanisms for effectiveness, efficiency and productivity. The interplay of work, people, and technology surround a concept called a *process* or *business process*—the vehicle which makes this interplay possible. When applied in the workplace, an understanding of these processes, their principles, and supporting techniques, will enhance the capability and effectiveness of individual workers and work teams, the leadership qualities of managers and executives, and the efficiency, productivity, competitiveness, and sustainability of organizations.

The practice of identifying, analyzing, measuring, and optimizing business processes is called *Business Process Management (BPM)*. The BPM discipline is going through an evolutionary cycle and is now gaining momentum because of the realization that effective and efficient business processes provide a competitive and sustainable advantage to organizations, while enhancing the capability of their workers and management. Traditionally, employees, technology, and of course, infrastructure have been accepted as valuable assets of an organization since the industrial revolution, but recognition of business processes as an asset—the underlying vehicle that enables other assets—continues to be a challenge in this information and knowledge age.

The definitions of an *asset* in Webster's Dictionary includes: "...the entire property of a person, association, corporation...", and "...the items on a balance sheet showing the book value of property owned..." Materials, technology, and infrastructure are well recognized as physical assets. Many organizations are finally recognizing their people as an asset, too, because of the skills and competencies that enable the business to operate. Thus, the notion of Human Capital has evolved in recent times as a critical resource, even though financially, employees are still recorded as a cost and sometimes measured based on "per square feet of occupied space". These assets are physical in nature and are readily identified. Therefore, it is easy for a corporation to assign a value to them in their books and records.

All of the traditional and physical assets of a corporation have little to no value unless they are utilized by a business process or processes. Of what value would factory space be if there were no manufacturing processes producing products? Of what value would a salesperson be if they weren't finding customers and selling products? Of what value would information systems be if they were not automatically executing a business process? Clearly, the answer is none. The value of these physical assets is realized only when they are assigned to or aligned with one or more business processes. Let me suggest, then, that business processes are not merely an asset, but a super asset; and without that super asset, no other asset is useful in an enterprise.

The processes are the link that "binds" other assets to produce products and services. However, unlike physical assets, which are visible to the naked eye, business processes are conceptual in nature and are, therefore, invisible. Sometimes, the processes are referred to as the "white space" on an organization chart of an enterprise. Therein lays the challenge for understanding and leveraging this super asset to maximize the potential of how work gets done.

Functional areas, such as manufacturing and finance, obscure our ability to see processes as "doing something". Functions are a vertical way of organizing units of work, skills, and allocating cost in a financial model. But products and services are delivered to customers, and interactions with other stakeholders take place by cutting across functional areas horizontally. Working documents such as procedures or so called standard operating procedures are simply one by-product of a business process understanding. These are only subsets of the whole process environment. By making decisions and performing based on that limited knowledge, management and workers sub optimize the value and potential of the whole asset. An organization that recognizes its processes as a critical asset, and therefore a critical resource, manages and optimizes this resource to achieve effectiveness, efficiency, and productivity. Such a business entity may be considered to be a process-centric organization.

Nasrudin is a folk hero of medieval origin. His role changes. Sometimes he is a sage, sometimes a fool; he is a courtier, beggar, physician, judge, and teacher. Whether his anecdotes are studied for their hidden wisdom, or enjoyed for their pungent humor, they are an enduring part of the world's cultural heritage. Let me use this story about Nine Donkeys on the following page to make a couple of points.

*Nasrudin*

Nasrudin once agreed to deliver nine donkeys to a farmer. The man who entrusted them to him counted them one by one, so that Nasrudin could be sure that there really were nine. While traveling, his attention was distracted by something on the side of the road. Nasrudin, sitting astride one of the animals, counted them again and again. He counted only eight donkeys. Panic-stricken, he jumped off, looked all over the place, and then counted them again. There were nine. Then he noticed a remarkable thing. When he was sitting on donkey-back, he could see only eight donkeys. When he dismounted, however, there were nine in full view. "This is the penalty", reflected Nasrudin, "for riding, when I should, no doubt, be walking behind the donkeys." "Did you have any difficulty getting them here?" asked the farmer when Nasrudin arrived, dusty and disheveled. "Not after I learned the trick of donkey-drivers, walk behind" said Nasrudin. "Before that, they were full of tricks."

There are some words of wisdom in this folk tale that are relevant to business processes: First, every worker and manager is "riding" on one or more processes all the time; they may not "see" them and don't recognize the vehicle that makes their work possible. By stepping aside, it is possible to see that their processes, and all other organizational processes, are one interconnected and interdependent whole. This understanding leads to more strategic thinking and planning to leverage the whole asset, which I will refer to as the *blueprint* of the organization. Some managers and executives recognize processes as assets and actively support and reward managing them. But, when they are replaced, new executives may not share their understanding and vision, proceeding to not only withdraw their support, but they also perpetuate the incompetence of not valuing their most critical resource. I have seen this cycle of process awareness and blindness repeated in organizations and among the business units within the same organization. I see these managers and executives as Nasrudins riding and dismounting the donkeys, unable to see the processes that run their business.

In this book, all of the relevant components will be put together in such a way that people at all levels of an organization, regardless of industry, understand the value of business processes and leverage these assets to transform their organizations to become process-centric. This would be a win-win for workers, managers, executives, and organizations, as a whole. Using a proven approach, I have identified steps for understanding and improving the business processes assets in a practical and methodical manner. This book will provide you with a foundation for practicing Business Process Management. It is my hope that when you have finished this book, you will see business processes and their value in a new light, and have a common language and tools that may immediately be applied to benefit your own competence, resulting in enhancing the capabilities of your organization.

Taking it one step further, this process know-how needs to be incorporated into college-level courses to enhance the capability of future leaders and should also be used by organizations as a core competency for training their executives, managers and workers.

Best wishes

Arjit "Artie" Mahal

The story of any enterprise begins with its business drivers. These drivers originate from one or more influences on the marketplace: *STEEPLE* – Social, Technological, Economical, Environmental, Political, Legal, and Ethical factors. We will use a simple way to view the high-level structure of an organization and how it responds to its business drivers – an *enterprise business model*.

A *business model* presents the concepts of the major components that make up an enterprise so that their interrelationships and dependencies can be understood, as illustrated in Figure 1.1. Let's take a closer look at Planning and Operations. The example used in this chapter pertains to the NewAge Foods business.

**Figure 1.1 Enterprise Business Model**

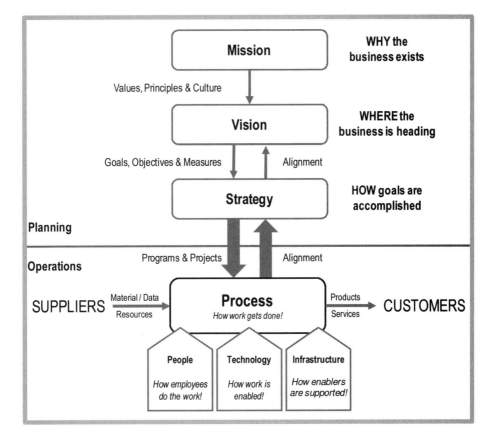

An enterprise responds to its drivers through two main functions within the business: Planning and Operations. Planning consists of the Mission, Vision, and Strategies of the business and remains stable over time. Operations are a collaboration of processes, people, and technology supported by an underlying infrastructure. It is dynamic and changes in response to business drivers.

## *Planning*

Planning consists of the Mission, Vision and Strategies of the business and remains stable over time.

### MISSION

The first element of the Planning component of the business model is the reason why the organization was created, its Mission. The Mission was established by the organization's owners, founders, and shareholders when the organization first came into being. It serves as a North Star to guide the enterprise. The Mission is generally stable and rarely changes over time. It drives the overall business model and is usually summarized in a succinct statement. See Figure 1.2 for the NewAge Foods Mission Statement.

**Figure 1.2 NewAge Foods Mission Statement**

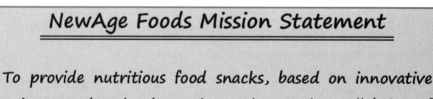

NewAge Foods Mission Statement

To provide nutritious food snacks, based on innovative science and technology, that enhance the well being of humans and provides moments of joy to individuals.

To successfully carry out the mission, values and guiding principles are developed. They serve as a check on business activities and individuals to ensure compliance with desired behaviors. These values and principles are reflected in all activities to ensure integrity and as a promise of the value the business wants to deliver to its customers and consumers. A corporate "Brand" is a manifestation of the mission and is supported by values and principles that promote and establish the unique behaviors the business wants to promote and be known for. For example, a corporation may want to be known as the employer of choice. To accomplish that, the employees would have to be treated as a true asset, given the opportunity to develop and grow, and be rewarded and recognized for their contributions. See Figure 1.3 for the NewAge Foods Values and Principles.

**Figure 1.3 NewAge Foods Values and Principles**

## NewAge Foods Values

We act in harmony with human nutritional needs and nutritional science. We do what is right and sustainable for nature. We accept personal responsibility for our products.

Principles:
- Quality in Products and Services
- Mutuality in all Stakeholder Relationships
- Efficiency in our Ways of Working

Collectively, the Mission, supported by Values and Principles, becomes the culture of the organization and permeates all aspects of the ways in which it functions.

## VISION

The next element in the business model is the Vision. The Vision is where the business is heading - what the organization would like to accomplish in the next three to seven years or more; a future state to which the business aspires to satisfy its Mission. In an enterprise, the stakeholders in the business - those who are impacted by, able to influence, the recipients of the business results, or all of the above, share collective expectations for the business and its products and services. The stakeholders include both the external and internal customers of an organization, its owners or shareholders, employees, suppliers, regulatory agencies, and even communities. The Vision is generally implemented incrementally and is adjusted over time in response to changing circumstances in the marketplace. The Vision is typically written in present-tense "as if the vision has been achieved." It provides Goals that are accomplished through measurable Objectives, which serve as the measures of success of the enterprise. See Figure 1.4 for the NewAge Foods Vision.

**Figure 1.4 NewAge Foods Vision**

## NewAge Foods Vision

NewAge Foods is a profitable, independent business with sustainable growth and a positive image. We lead the field in healthy, nutritious, and tasty snacks, with an ongoing pipeline of new products consistent with proven food science technology. We are recognized as the best place to work in the country and to do business with by both customers and suppliers.

This vision statement is the future state of where NewAge wants to be. It is written in present tense. A vision statement should be written in this form to inspire the employees as if the organization has already "reached" the desired state. The Vision is used to "see the invisible" and promote confidence in that journey.

The Goals deduced from the elements of the Vision are the end towards which effort is directed. The effort is the Strategy. Strategies, then, have specific Objectives that determine end of action, when achieved. The measure of that end-of-action or success is a *Key Performance Indicator (KPI)*. The management activity of ensuring that the Objectives, their Strategies, and Goals continue to be in sync with the desired Vision is called Alignment. Organizational management is held accountable for "forward" execution of and alignment with the Vision. Note: In some organizations, the term Objective is used instead of Goal; and likewise, the term Goal may be used in place of Objective. See Figure 1.5 for the NewAge Foods Goals.

**Figure 1.5 NewAge Foods Goals**

## NewAge Foods Goals

Based on phrases from our Vision Statement, we have the following Goals:

| Phrase from Vision ⟶ | Goals |
|---|---|
| profitable business | Return on Investment |
| sustainable growth | Increased Market Share |
| positive image | Brand Recognition |
| healthy & tasty snacks | Product Positioning |
| pipeline of new products | Product Segment Extension |
| food-science technology | Best in Class Practices |
| best place to work | Employee Satisfaction/Retention |
| best company to buy from | Enhanced Customer Relationship |
| best company to do business with | Enhanced Supplier Relationship |

For example, take a Goal of an organization's Vision: "Increase Market Share" for their products and services. One of the strategies would be to identify and build relationships and sell to new customers. One of the objectives of that strategy would be to *Increase Market Share for Organic Snacks in the North East by 10%*. This expected outcome would be the KPI that would demonstrate whether the vision is being achieved and to what degree. The resulting numbers are one factor by which success may be measured.

Each of these Goals, when appropriately executed through well-defined strategies, would drive measurable Objectives. See Figure 1.6 for the NewAge Foods Objectives and KPIs.

**Figure 1.6 NewAge Foods Objectives and KPIs**

<u>**NewAge Foods Objectives & KPIs**</u>

**Objective:** Increase Market Share for Organic Snacks in the Northeast

**KPI:** 7%  Increase in Sales

**Objective:** Provide Product Segment Extension by One New Product in Ensuing Year

**KPI:**  One Successful Product Launch

**Objective:** Increase Employees Engagement

**KPI:**  90th Percentile of the organizations with the highest employee engagement score

The old wisdom of "what is measured gets done" is at the heart of every business, its viability, and success. The professional practice around this topic can be referred to as Performance Management. The factors which are critical for the survival of the business are identified, measured, and acted upon when found unbalanced. Typically, these are about customer and finance. In process-centric organizations, where the processes are viewed as an asset, there would be a "seat at the table" for the business processes, as depicted in the proposed balanced scorecard diagram in Figure 1.7. The dashboard of an organization is like the dials in the cockpit of an aircraft; and the measure of altitude, wind factor, gasoline, weight, weather, and distance are the data displayed as the scorecard. Just as the aircraft measures must be balanced for it to safely arrive at its destination, so is the scorecard designed for arriving at the destination of the business—the Vision.

**Figure 1.7 Alignment of Performance Measures**

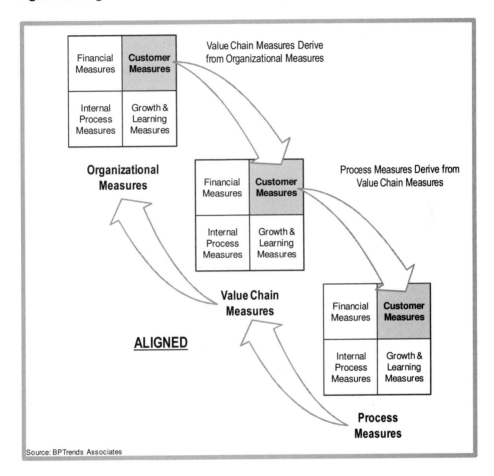

Source: BPTrends Associates

## STRATEGY

A Strategy is a methodical approach for achieving the Objectives established in the Vision. It aligns the elements of Vision, Goals, Objectives, and Measures to create actions for directing the Operations of the organization. These actions are called **Programs or Programs for Change**. See Figure 1.8 for the NewAge Foods **Strategy**.

**Figure 1.8 NewAge Foods Strategy**

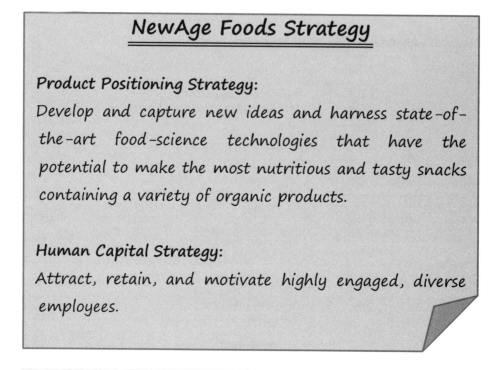

## NewAge Foods Strategy

**Product Positioning Strategy:**

Develop and capture new ideas and harness state-of-the-art food-science technologies that have the potential to make the most nutritious and tasty snacks containing a variety of organic products.

**Human Capital Strategy:**

Attract, retain, and motivate highly engaged, diverse employees.

## *Programs and Projects*

Programs are the means by which Strategies are implemented. They bring about change in the operation of the business by enhancing the capabilities, products, and services offered by the enterprise to its stakeholders. The Programs constitute Projects, which are a means of developing and implementing changes through a logical set of work elements using resources such as people, money, and equipment. For example, in NewAge Foods, to develop a snack from a specific grain would be a Project; the setup of infrastructure to do multiple such projects would be a Program. Leadership is assigned to the Programs and Projects to marshal needed resources and deliver required results. Program Management Office (PMO), is the organizational entity that manages Programs and Projects. Traditionally, PMO has been "project focused", but it needs to mature towards "program focus" that requires a higher-level of management sophistication in the governance of an organization. See Figures 1.9 and 1.10 for the NewAge Foods Programs.

**Figures 1.9 NewAge Foods Product Positioning Programs**

## NewAge Foods Product Positioning Strategy

**Program 1:** Develop snacks from organic grains produced by local farmers; create the supporting logistics and organizational structure for success.

**Program 2:** Develop customized snacks for specific usage such as cookies for diabetics; build marketing, production, and sales organization around the new offering.

**Program 3:** Partner with the scientific community and grocery industry to promote the value of the brand; support that initiative with underlying processes to enhance the value of that brand.

**Figures 1.10 NewAge Foods Human Capital Programs**

## NewAge Foods Human Capital Strategy

**Program 1:**    Define, design, and implement an effective, competency-based organization structure.

**Program 2:**    Establish performance-driven compensation and enhance Human Capital through quality acquisition and development of talent based on organizational core competencies.

**Program 3:**    Define criteria for and develop high performing work teams through the integration of team building attributes required of each project in the organization.

## *Operations*

Operations are fundamentally the workings of all parts of an organization in support of its Mission. The components of the Operations part of the business are: People, Processes, Technology, and Infrastructure. The success of the Operations of an enterprise is assessed through measures and their metrics to ensure the performance of all parts meet expectations. As mentioned in the Introduction, People, Technology, and Infrastructure are the traditional assets and resources deployed to conduct the Operations of an organization. However, business processes—the "invisible" asset, are the ones that actually make it possible to deliver products and services to the end customers or stakeholders. Thus, people do not deliver products, and services; people enable or execute the processes that deliver products and services. Employees are assigned to functional areas of the business based on their skills and the type of work expected from them. This is a legacy of the industrial age and accounting-driven business models wherein people with similar skills are managed through functional "silos". Work, however, is actually done cross-functionally, as depicted in Figure 1.11.

**Figure 1.11 Business Functions and Processes**

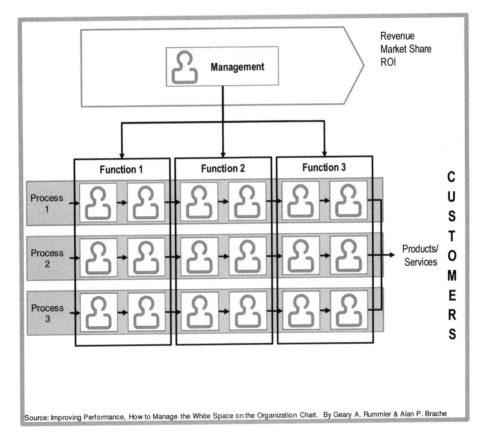

Source: Improving Performance, How to Manage the White Space on the Organization Chart. By Geary A. Rummler & Alan P. Brache

Figure 1.11 raises the question: If work is performed "horizontally" to deliver value to the customer, then why are businesses organized "vertically"? The answer is not simple. While process-centric companies are trying to organize around processes, a more common model is a matrix organizational structure in which the partnership of two disciplines, Business Process Management and Organization Development, is critical.

## PROCESS

The simple definition of a business process is: "how work gets done." It is a series of activities or tasks that are performed together to produce a defined result. Typically, a process has inputs which are transformed into outputs and outcomes. The inputs can be data, material, or state of "things" such as a customer order getting transformed into a fulfilled order. In simple terms, a process is triggered by an event, governed by some rules using relevant knowledge, and executed through people using enabling technology and supporting infrastructure, such as facilities. See Figure 1.12.

**Figure 1.12 Process Overview**

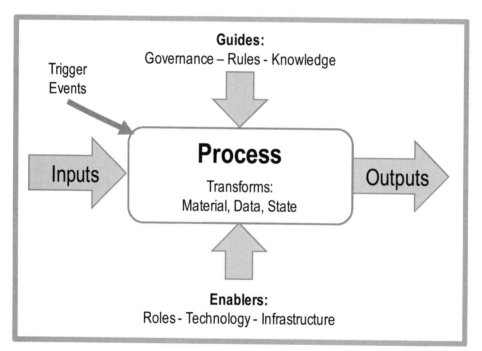

All work performed in a business may be classified into management, production, and support. Management processes include the development of strategic plans, research and development, and regulatory compliance. In manufacturing, the production processes include procurement of raw materials, its conversion to finished goods, and the logistics of delivering the goods to customers. Support processes include the recruitment and deployment of employees, installation and deployment of equipment, and development and deployment of information technology applications. In a service industry, the production processes would include development of new offerings, marketing new offerings, contracting for delivery of services, delivering services, and invoicing to the customers. It is worth noting that in an enterprise, it is the production or core processes that bring in the revenue from customers and consumers, while management and support processes are typically overhead, in terms of simple accounting. Therefore, management tends to put more funding into the core processes and attempts to minimize the costs of support processes. The strategies are executed through business processes and therefore, these two must be in alignment. See Figure 1.13 for the NewAge Foods Business Processes.

**Figure 1.13 NewAge Foods Business Processes**

## NewAge Foods Processes

**Management :**
Develop Business Strategy.
Provide Legal and Regulatory Compliance.
Monitor Trends and Benchmark.

**Production/Core :**
Market to Customers.
Convert Raw Material into Finished Goods.
Invoice and Settle with the Customer.

**Support:**
Provide Competent Employees.
Provide Financial Services.
Provide Information Technology Services.

## PEOPLE

If process is defined as "how work gets done", people are defined as "how people/employees do the work". People or employees with the required skills, competencies, and experience are referred to as Human Capital. The overall professional practice of managing the Human Capital of an organization through effective policies and practices is called Organization Development (OD), which is typically organized under a function known as Human Resources. Organizational design, a subset of OD, is the practice of designing the optimal structure for accomplishing work and compensating employees based on their respective roles and performance. The employees' roles are aligned to the business processes based on the required skills and competencies needed for the successful execution of the process. Note: an employee has no value to the organization until s/he is assigned to one or more processes. See Figure 1.14 for the NewAge Foods People Roles.

**Figure 1.14 NewAge Foods People Roles**

## NewAge Foods People Roles

**Management Roles:** Chief Executive Officer, Business Planning Director, Chief Financial Officer.

**Production Roles:** Brand Manager, Sales Account Manager, Production Operator, Customer Service Representative.

**Support Roles:** Human Resources Manager, Systems Analyst, Facilities Manager.

## TECHNOLOGY

Technology, data, and systems are enablers of an organization. Data, when transformed by a process, becomes information. The information may be recorded in a variety of ways, including on paper, electronically in a document or spreadsheet, or in a data store. Data and processes have a unique relationship - without data, a process cannot create information, and conversely, without process, the data has no means of being transformed into information. See Figure 1.15 for the NewAge Foods Data, Systems, and Technology.

**Figure 1.15 NewAge Foods Data, Systems, and Technology**

### NewAge Foods Data & Systems & Technology

Data:
    Customer Name and Address
    Number of Active Customers
    Invoice Amount

Systems:
    Order Processing Application
    Accounts Receivable Application
    Accounts Payable Application

Technology:
    Manufacturing Production Lines
    Robotics
    Enterprise Resource Planning (ERP)

If a business process is the "body", then information is the "nervous system". Data itself has a life cycle: datum is transformed into information when it interacts with a process. Information, in turn, is the foundation for building organizational knowledge. The automation of business processes, along with the supporting data and information, become systems applications such as Accounts

Payable, Product Ordering, and Invoicing. Technology may include the production lines, robotics, equipment, information technology, and other production mechanisms.

## INFRASTRUCTURE

Infrastructure is the organizational capability that supports other enablers such as processes, people, and technology. Infrastructure may include the buildings, technical platforms, communications, and energy. For supporting processes, infrastructure includes facilities, offices, and factories. For supporting people, it includes space, desks, and chairs. For supporting technology, infrastructure includes hardware, software, and equipment. See Figure 1.16 for the NewAge Foods Infrastructure.

**Figure 1.16 NewAge Foods Infrastructure**

## NewAge Foods Infrastructure

Buildings, Facilities, Roads, Hardware & Software, Internet, Electricity, and Energy.

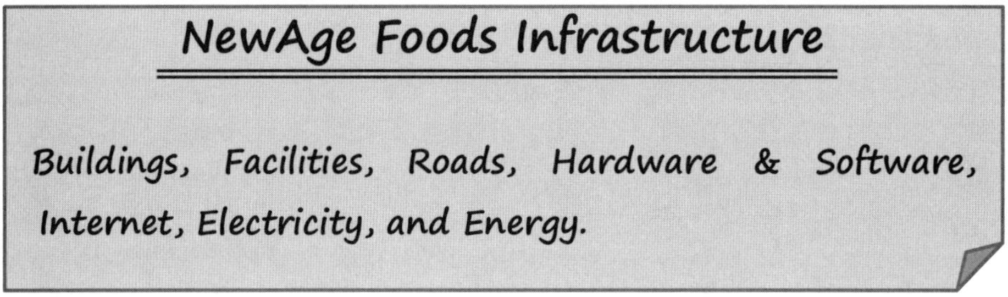

### Business Complexity

All components of an organization directly or indirectly have one common denominator - processes. Business processes are how doing business and running the business is accomplished; they are the "throbbing heart" of the business, fulfilling its mission and achieving its vision. For an organization to survive and thrive, the complexity of and interaction among all business processes must be optimized for performance and aligned with other assets, such as money, people, equipment, systems, and infrastructure. All organizational components, irrespective of the industry, exist in relation to the business processes. An understanding of the complexity of an organization, illustrated in Figure 1.17, by all workers, managers, and executives is the basis for business know-how, the core competency that makes an organization effective and efficient, and for its employees, provides the opportunity for development and professional advancement.

**Figure 1.17 Business Process Complexities (The "Enterprise Hairball")**

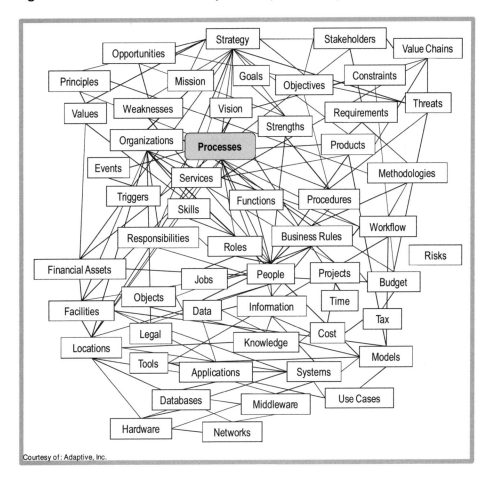

Courtesy of: Adaptive, Inc.

## Key Points

- In an organization, the Mission describes the reason for its purpose and existence. The Vision defines the future state that the organization aspires to achieve. And the Strategies are the approach and actions by which the Vision is achieved. Strategies are implemented through the execution of processes.

- Business processes produce and deliver products and services in an organization; people, technology and infrastructure are enablers to the processes.

- In the complexity of any organization, processes are the most common denominator where all objects, concepts, services, and products, connect and have purpose of being.

- Understanding the business model and its complexities in an organization promotes work effectiveness and thus delivers performance. This know-how creates business acumen, which must be established as a core competency for all employees.

# CHAPTER 2
## Business Process Hierarchy

Business processes may be decomposed from a higher-level of abstraction to more detailed lower-level steps. Their components are arranged in a hierarchical structure. While each individual business process represents "how work gets done", at the organization level these processes collectively add up to a common blueprint of "how the overall work gets done". The technical term for this blueprint is Business Process Architecture. This chapter describes a simple process and the process hierarchy and its purpose.

A business process receives one or more inputs which trigger the process to do something. It then transforms the inputs and produces one or more outputs that may then be input to another process or simply be the final outcome. The source of inputs may be one or more stakeholders or other processes. Likewise, the destination of the outputs may be one or more stakeholders or other processes. The stakeholders are those individuals, entities, or organizational entities that have a vested interest in the process and either contribute input to or are the recipients of the output. Recall Figure 1.12, Process Overview, from the previous chapter.

Consider a process such as "Bake-a-Cake", in Figure 2.1. The ingredients are the inputs. They are blended together according to a recipe and are transformed into a baked cake as the output. A business event triggers or initiates the process to perform some action or transformation. For example, a family member's birthday would trigger the Bake-a-Cake Process to prepare for the celebration.

**Figure 2.1 Bake-a-Cake Process Example**

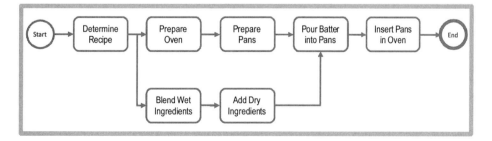

There are two other dimensions to the process format - guides and enablers. Guides govern the process but are not "consumed" by it. These include management of the process, strategies, policies, practices including business rules, and the knowledge needed to execute the process. One example of process strategy is the allocated budget, a practice would be the cake recipe, and knowledge would include previously learned skills for combining the ingredients the right way to make the best cake possible. Enablers are the "reusable tools" that constitute people roles, data, systems or mechanisms, and infrastructure. The baker is an example of a role. The bowls, pots, and pans may be thought of as the "systems", a recipe file as the data/information store, and an example of the infrastructure would be the kitchen and electric power for the operation of the oven. For simplicity, the guides may be referred to as the "Rules", and the enablers as the "Tools". Irrespective of the type of work to be done, an individual process has inputs, guides, enablers, and outputs. Typically, the guides are outputs of some management process such as **Plan Business Strategy**, and the enablers are outputs of some support process such as **Develop Organization Design**. In Chapter 4, *Anatomy of a Process*, the structure of a process will be explored further.

## *Process Hierarchy*

A process may be broken into smaller steps that are referred to as sub processes, activities, tasks, or work instructions, as shown in Figure 2.2. There is an art to determining the content of each level of the hierarchy so that it effectively communicates the purpose and definition of the process. The levels of the hierarchy should be standardized in an organization to promote a common language and understanding of the level of detail in consideration for a specific purpose.

**Figure 2.2 Process Hierarchy Guide**

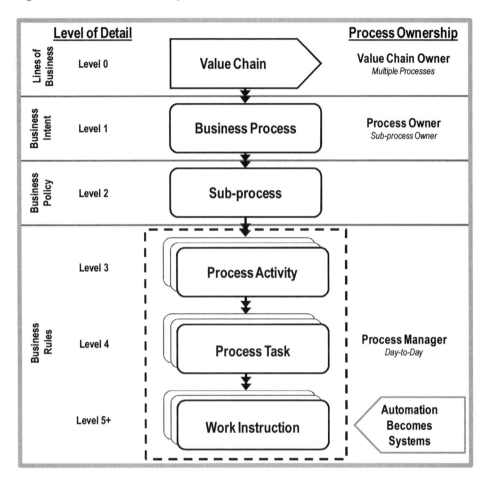

## LEVEL 0

The highest level of the hierarchy, or Level 0, typically refers to the *Value Chain*. A value chain represents one or more sets of processes that, at an organization level, convert inputs into outputs, thereby delivering some unique value to its customers and stakeholders. The value chains may be thought of as unique ways of organizing the lines of business or products and services to ensure performance and success. For an automobile manufacturer, one value chain may be the production of sedans and another, the production of school buses. In NewAge Foods, one value chain is for manufacturing and selling wholesale to brokers and retail to customers, whereas another value chain is for a mail-order business that sells directly to consumers. The success of these value chains, the sum total of all the resources allocated to a given value chain measured against their sales and revenue, helps an organization decide how to position their products and services for success.

## LEVEL 1

Level 1 contains the highest-level management processes representing the Business Intent—the creation and delivery of products and services. There may be anywhere from 20 to 30 processes at this level, depending on how management sees their business. Typically, senior executives are responsible for managing one or more of the processes that touch their traditional functional areas. Since the outputs of some processes are inputs to others, the seamless integration of inputs/outputs in cross-functional areas is the responsibility of the management team. The notion of make the "functional silos" work begins at this level of the organization. Level 1 processes are used for developing business vision, measures, and strategies, and ensuring regulatory compliance is effective. In addition, determining the viability of mergers and acquisitions with prospective companies by mapping the high-level processes is a major benefit of identifying the Level 1 business processes. Some examples of Level 1 processes in NewAge Foods would be: **Plan Business Strategy**, **Forecast Demand**, **Market to Customer**, and **Provide Capable Employees**.

## LEVEL 2

The processes resulting from decomposing the Level 1 processes to the next lower-level of detail are referred to as Level 2 processes. The purpose of this level is to further establish ways of working and to determine business policies. Each level of the decomposition contains processes, but they may also be referred to as sub-processes because they are components of higher level processes. The rule of thumb is that when you decompose a business process, it could have five to nine sub-processes (Rule of 7 +/- 2). If there are fewer than five, then either the detail is not sufficient or you've reached the lowest level of decomposition for that process. If there are more than seven or nine, then it is likely that the processes are a little too detailed. Decomposing processes and keeping them at an understandable level of detail is a skill that comes with experience; it is not an exact science. Naming processes by using a structure of Verb-Noun helps in this exercise and will be covered in a later chapter. Let's look at an example of how one Level 1 process for NewAge Foods, **Provide Capable Employees,** leads to ways of working and business policies, in Figure 2.3.

**Figure 2.3 Process Decomposition**

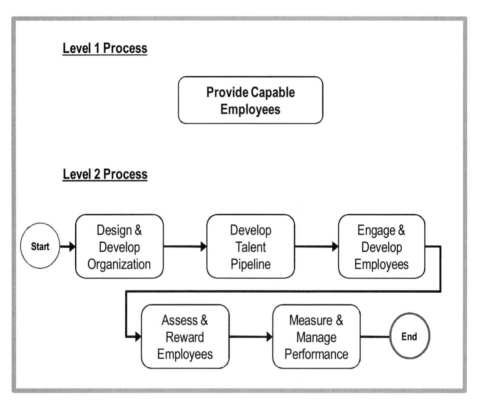

As you can see, **Provide Capable Employees** was decomposed into five Level 2 processes. In each of these processes, the ways of operating and business policies are established based on the values, and thus the culture, of the organization. The business policies are implemented in lower-level processes in the form of Business Rules. Here are some examples of business policies for our example processes:

- **Design and Develop Organization** – policy on organization structure including span of control
- **Develop Talent Pipeline** – policy on acquiring talent externally versus developing from within the organization

- **Measure and Manage Performance** – policy on metrics for measuring and establishing reward and recognition of employees.

## LEVEL 3 AND LOWER

Each Level 2 process may be further decomposed into its respective Level 3 processes, meaning a more finely detailed set of processes. Again, each Level 2 process may have from five to nine Level 3 sub-processes. This starts to be the operational transactional work where process policies supported by data rules and business rules are implemented: who does what to whom, why, when, and where. When we look at an operational procedure, it is typically a document which references roles, tasks, or work instructions to describe how work gets done. Thus, a Level 3 business process is a "child" and a "grandchild" of some organizational processes. Employees sometimes have difficulty conceptualizing, and have a hard time seeing the procedure as a document describing steps of a process. Employees who don't understand the value of process "boxes and arrows" as the basis for procedures, have difficulty in understanding the value of process analysis. This is another reason for educating employees at all levels of the organization in process-orientation.

The business policies developed in the Level 2 processes are translated into process policies and detailed data and business rules in Level 3 and below. Processes in Level 4 may be referred to as *Tasks* and at Level 5 as *Work Instructions*. Level 4 may also be referred to as *Activity* and Level 5 as a *Task*. This raises an important consideration - how to label these levels of detail in your organization. It is not a question of what is right, but rather a matter of establishing a consistent, common language for communication.

Occasionally, processes may have to be decomposed lower than Level 5 (sometimes to levels 7 and more in military processes, for example). You must seriously consider whether or not there is a real need for lower levels of detail or if there is a way to consolidate some process steps into a higher-level of abstraction.

Business processes may be represented by a set of diagrams accompanied by textual descriptions. An overview of the diagrams will be given in a later chapter. Standard Operating Procedures (SOP) are merely an amalgamation of lower-level process activities and tasks mapped against people roles and data and business rules. This concept is not very well understood by business people, or even by analysts.

## *How Information Systems are Born*

While any level of the process hierarchy may be implemented as a business application system using information technology, transactional systems are created by automating processes at Level 3 and below. This is where the "rubber meets the road". Examples of transactional systems include Order Processing, Recruiting and Hiring Employees, and Payroll Processing. It is sometimes difficult for both business and IT personnel to understand that systems are born by automating processes. I remember an incident where a senior IT executive, upon being advised to define business processes before developing systems, made this statement: "We are in the business of developing systems, what do we have to do with processes?" This is another reason for improving awareness and education at all levels of the organization.

It is clear, then, that business application requirements must be defined from the top of the hierarchy of processes down to lower levels of process before systems are developed or software packages implemented. Consider the implications of starting the construction of your home on a plot of land without the blueprints; this is no different. Business processes are the "drawings" of business requirements upon which the "construction" of systems must take place. Any shortcuts to this will invariably result in false starts, rework, increased cost, frustration, and possibly even failure.

## Key Points

- Business processes have an inherent hierarchy from a high level of abstraction to progressively lower levels of detail. Each level has a purpose: Value Chain defines the line of business and alignment of producing products and services and allocation of resources for the success of the enterprise. Level 1 helps in developing business intent. Level 2 helps in establishing business policies. And Levels 3 and below are where peoples' roles are organized to perform activities, tasks, and work instructions. Procedures or Standard Operating Procedures (SOP) are an amalgamation and derivative of lower-level processes.

- Identifying processes and creating hierarchies of them is an art, rather than an exact science. Experience, wisdom, and effective leadership on the part of management leads to organizing the workings of the organization into business process assets and leveraging them for effective business changes and operations. If a process has a "child" then it is a "parent" or "super-process"; if it has a "parent" then it is a "sub-process".

- Automation of specific business processes, serving specific business purposes, gives birth to IT systems. Transactional applications systems are typically created at Level 3 and below, where people and process interact. Management applications systems are typically created for Levels 1 and 2. No automation should be undertaken until the business process has been designed for optimal use.

If we consider all the business processes at all levels, from the top to the bottom of the overall hierarchy, there are likely to be hundreds, if not thousands, of processes in any organization. Therefore, it is imperative that all business processes be organized in an effective manner for understanding, communicating, and optimizing performance of "how all work gets done". This is achieved by creating an organizational blueprint, which is defined at "37 thousand feet"— the highest level of abstraction, and then drilled down to the desired levels of detail. It is similar to having an architect draw the blueprint of a house, beginning with a landscape view, then drilling down to the drawings of the room layouts, and finally, to the definition of plumbing, electric wiring, and various infrastructure details. Process Blueprint is to the organization what a structural Blueprint is to a building.

We make every effort to ensure that our homes are constructed for living-effectiveness and have efficiencies in the utilization of energy, while still being fully functional. In the context of the business processes of an organization, the blueprint that contains all the "drawings" of "how work gets done" is technically called a Business Process Architecture.

## *Business Process Blueprint Explanation*

A Business Process Architecture is typically defined for an Organization-in-Focus (OIF) - the entire organization at the corporate-level, or a business unit, or a specific functional area such as finance or marketing and sales. Ideally, the Process Architecture should be defined at the enterprise-level. Sometimes that is not practical or cost effective due to lack of management support, so functional-level Process Architecture may be defined with the intent of retrofitting it into an organizational Process Architecture at a later date. I will be interchanging the terms Business Process Architecture and the Business Process Blueprint.

Driven by the Mission, Vision, and Strategies, the Business Process Blueprint is specified in a set of diagrams that are accompanied by detailed text to the desired level of detail. The diagrams are visual representations of processes and are intended to facilitate effective communication and act as a tool for dialogue in running the business at an optimal level.

The Business Process Blueprint should be forward looking and aligned with the vision, strategic objectives and goals of the organization. It should represent where the organization wants to go, with an eye towards transforming from its current state to a future state, based on priorities and strategies.

This is a macro-level view of how work gets done in an Organization-in-Focus (OIF). Ideally, the OIF should start at the Enterprise-level, working top-down to decompose to the lowest-level processes. However, the reality is management may not understand the value of creating an Enterprise-level because they don't see this invisible asset. This makes a case for educating all employees in the value of processes—starting at the top of the organization.

It is perfectly valid to create a Business Process Blueprint for an organization unit if a division or function manager understands its value and has the will and the means to take a process-centric approach towards managing their business area. The organization unit would then be the OIF for the context of the Blueprint. For example, the NewAge Foods Company's Vice President of Human Resources may sponsor the creation of a Business Process Blueprint for the Human Resources area. While creating a Blueprint for a functional area, a silo, is not ideal, it is better to have one organization unit taking a process-centric approach than none at all. It is to be hoped that eventually other organization units would follow suit and that management will decide to create an enterprise blueprint that integrates the lower-level blueprints. The parts will make up the whole. Understand, however, that in an architecture that is developed from the bottom up, the cross-functional and cross-process design may be sub-optimal.

Let's discuss the philosophy of building and defining a Business Process Blueprint: The Blueprint must be stakeholder driven. The stakeholders are those individuals or entities who have a vested interest in the success of, and are the beneficiaries of the OIF. The stakeholders may be internal and/or external. The Blueprint begins with the perspective of key stakeholders such as customers, owners, shareholders, suppliers, and employees.

While there is no one standard for visually depicting a Blueprint, I have found the diagram depicted in Figure 3.1 to be a best practice.

**Figure 3.1 Business Process Architecture (Blueprint)**

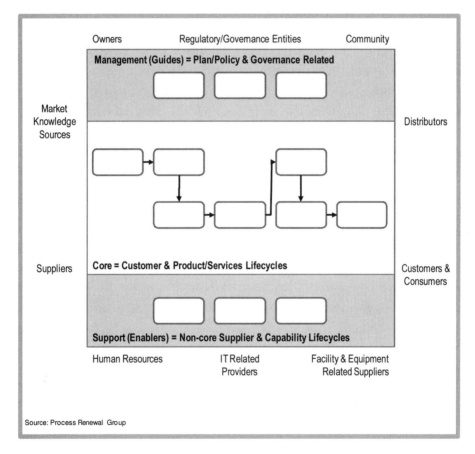

There are three distinct types of processes in the Blueprint: Management processes (Guiding processes), Core processes (Production processes), and Support processes (Enabling processes). As shown in the template of the Blueprint in Figure 3.1, the

Management, or Guiding processes are documented at the top, Core processes, where Input-Process-Output takes place, in the middle, and Support or Enabler processes are at the bottom. This is aligned with the process structure we saw earlier in this chapter and helps promote a common language in the organization.

Management processes are those which govern the organization, such as **Develop Strategic Plans**, and **Monitoring and Manage Performance**. These processes provide direction to OIF and are accountable for its overall performance and regulatory compliance.

Core processes produce and deliver products and services as outputs and achieve the strategic intent of the organization, which may include increasing market share, revenue, and visibility of their brands. In other words, the transformation from raw materials to finished goods and their delivery to customers would be recognized as Core processes. They connect to the customers, consumers, and clients on one end, and the suppliers of the raw materials on the other end. The raw materials and finished goods are generically defined here as a concept and differ, of course, depending on the nature of the OIF's business.

Support processes are defined as those processes which provide resources to the Core processes for their operation. Examples include **Provide Human Resources**, **Provide Financial Services**, **Provide Facilities Support**, and **Provide Information Technology**. These may also be viewed as the reusable resources of the organization. For example, the roles in the organization or systems are reused. While Core processes are at the heart of the organization and generate revenue, the Support processes are mostly a cost, but a necessary cost.

It makes sense, therefore, for an organization to always put more resources behind the Core processes and try to cut costs in the Support processes. Many organizations have Shared Services for HR and Finance for that very reason. The Management processes are, of course, critical for providing direction, measuring progress, managing risk, and ensuring compliance for regulatory entities.

There are numerous relationships among all the processes in the Blueprint, but at this macro-level, only the significant inputs and outputs are represented to show the integration and various touch points.

The Business Process Blueprint in Figure 3.1 represents Level 1 processes. For any organization, irrespective of their size, it would have anywhere from 20 to 30 processes at the enterprise-level. Again, this is the craft of defining macro-level processes and reflects the preferences of management for the visual representation. A collection of these processes may form one or more value chains, with the value chains likely to share some common processes--particularly the support processes. Each of these processes should have descriptions that include all the attributes that define the process. The overall Process Architecture of an enterprise will have hundreds of processes, representing all levels in the hierarchies. For effective management of these processes, the architecture may be divided into corporate architecture and operational architecture.

## *Corporate and Operational Process Maps*

Corporate Process Maps include the Value Chains and Level 1 and 2 processes. At this level, the processes are more stable and provide direction for business change initiatives. Management owns the Corporate Process Maps collectively and assigns process ownership accountabilities at value chain levels and processes. Operational Process Maps, which are derived from and are in alignment with the Corporate Process Maps, support the business operations and change projects. They are relatively dynamic in nature and are the main users of Information Technology. Operational management owns these processes, under the direction of the process owners from Value Chains and Levels 1 and 2 processes.

Let's review the NewAge Foods Company's Business Process Blueprint and examine the benefits of Corporate Business Process Maps and Process Architecture, in general. Figure 3.2 shows that the core processes of NewAge Foods are a collection of processes, in sequence, which produce and deliver snacks and collect money. There are two value chains: Produce-to-Stock, which involves selling to the customers that are retail stores and also to end consumers, and Build-to-Order, selling to consumers through mail-order. The value chains in this example share some common processes such as **Forecast Market Demand** and **Perform Research and Development**. This approach leverages the advantage of common capability while containing cost to the organization. The management processes are displayed at the top and the support processes at the bottom. While there are many inputs and outputs all through this process blueprint, only the core processes are shown with summary level flows among the processes. This simplifies the readability of the map. Each of the processes on the map would have definitions documented for common understanding and communication—including assignment of process owners.

**Figure 3.2 Business Process Architecture of NewAge Foods**

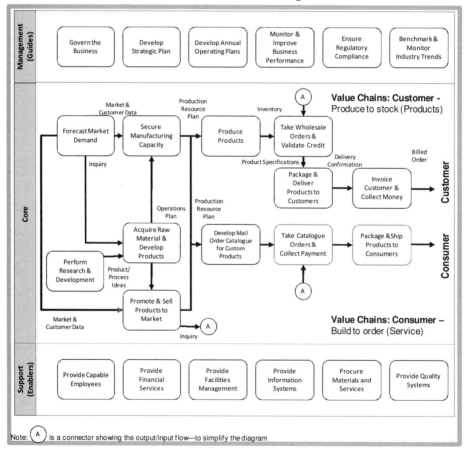

Figure 3.3 shows an example of Level 2 decomposition of one of the core processes.

**Figure 3.3 Core process Forecast Market Demand expanded**

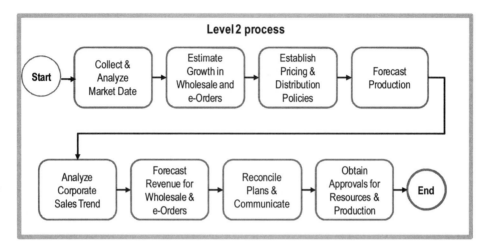

A process blueprint such as this facilitates management thinking for strategic intent and transformation of the business towards the desired vision. The use of this map and the supporting details helps management in:

- Developing strategies and providing direction to business operations. This could be a starting point for major business change initiatives, including mergers and acquisitions. It is also a tool for ensuring regulatory compliance and risk mitigation by establishing process ownerships.
- Establishing process ownership for the accountability of managing performance through meaningful measurements. This is enabled by measuring and rewarding the process owners on the success of their processes, not just on the functional areas they manage.
- Optimizing cost and effectiveness to ensure better return on investment and measurement of each value chain in terms of profitability and viability.
- Defining the competency needs for business operations and establishing a talent pipeline to ensure achieving human performance through appropriate management of the human capital.

- Aligning various capabilities of the organization such as brands, products and services, strategies, processes, information and knowledge, human resources, technology, and facilities.

## *Insights*

Just as the blueprint of a building is essential for constructing, maintaining, and changing parts of the structure, a blueprint of any business is essential for managing the parts of the business and its operations. In particular, the business process blueprint facilitates business understanding and highlights areas to focus on for improvement and optimization. Simply put, the business process blueprint defines an overall view of "what work gets done" and provides directions for "how all work must be done". When understood and utilized well, this is a powerful tool for the induction and training of employees, thereby expediting their learning curve in the organization and enabling them to be productive more quickly.

The blueprint is the basis for management to assign accountabilities, establish performance measures to monitor progress, and prioritize areas of improvement. For mergers and acquisitions, this blueprint may serve as the basis for a meaningful dialogue to ensure alignment between the business' core competencies. Management support is critical for the creation and use of an enterprise process blueprint because the funding of prioritized processes begins there. Savvy management has the foresight to see business processes as an asset of the enterprise and knows how to use them to help the business survive and thrive in its mission.

When business processes and their blueprints are not valued as an asset, employees at all levels of an organization spend endless hours in unproductive discussions and assumptions. Unfortunately, this is very common in the business environment. And in some cases, one set of management begins to see the value of this asset and thus initiates the business process management discipline, but when management changes, the new "leadership" ignores and sometimes even cuts it from the budget out of ignorance. It may be argued that businesses have been successful without the help of organized and managed business process, but they can be more progressive, productive, and competitive in today's fast changing business environment if they realize the value of the processes and the benefit of managing them.

Then what can business managers and knowledge workers in an organization do? In your own areas of the business, create a process blueprint by understanding and documenting how work is getting done and how it should be done. While it won't be aligned with blueprints created in other areas of the business (if there are any), your area will be able to demonstrate the value it provides. And maybe that will be enough to encourage other parts of the business to jump on the bandwagon. Henry Ford is believed to have said, "Take care of the pennies and the dollars will take care of themselves."

Note that there are several industry based process architectures or frameworks available in the market place, which can give a "jump start" to any architecture development effort. One, in particular, the Process Classification Framework, is a generic, cross-industry architecture that can be used by any industry to get ideas for processes, their names, and structure. It is available through the American Productivity & Quality Center (APQC) website: www.apqc.org.

## Key Points

- A process defines how work gets done, and a business process architecture/blueprint describes what those processes are. The logical collection of all business processes in an enterprise defines how work gets done in the overall organization. This logical view is the Enterprise Business Process Blueprint for understanding and optimizing the workings of the organization. Its technical name is Enterprise Business Process Architecture.

- A Business Process Blueprint is to a business what a structural Blueprint is to the construction and maintenance of a building.

- An Enterprise Business Process Blueprint contains the Value Chain(s), Levels 1 and 2 processes, and is strategic in focus. Levels 3 and below are also a subset of the Blueprint, but they are more prone to transactional business change and thus are project driven.

- Creation, maintenance, and governance of a Business Process Blueprint and its supporting infrastructure are overhead to an organization. Their value cannot be easily calculated in terms of Return on Investment (ROI), so management should not require it for this asset. Business Processes are no less an asset than the traditional assets that are considered overhead. It is no different than having a human resources group to manage people assets and a financial group to manage the monetary assets of the organization, neither of which is required to justify ROI.

# CHAPTER 4
## Anatomy of a Process

In this chapter, we will explore the "anatomy of a business process". I will show you the anatomy of a process part by part, and the value these provide in understanding and analyzing business processes. In the previous chapter, we covered the business process blueprint, which is composed of a set of business processes. Here, we will take one of those processes and become familiar with what's inside its own structure and gain an understanding of the value it provides. The process structure in Figure 4.1 is referred to as the Burlton Model.

**Figure 4.1 Anatomy of a Business Process - "Burlton Model"**

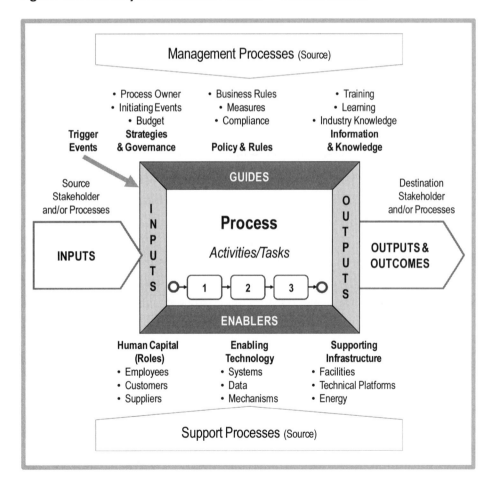

The definition of a business process is: A series of steps that produce something of value—products or services—for its stakeholders. It is simply "how work gets done". The stakeholders are those individuals or entities who have a vested interest in the process and would be the beneficiaries of the process results. The stakeholders can be both internal and external to the Organization-in-Focus.

A process is typically represented by a diagram with supporting textual information. The name of a process is usually made up of a *verb-noun* combination and it may also have a unique identifier for reference. For example, a high-level process such as **Forecast Demand** may be assigned the 1.0 identifier. When further decomposed into its sub processes, they will be identified as 1.1, 1.2, and so on. There are various objects that make up the structure of a process.

A process is initiated by an *Event*. It receives *Inputs,* which are transformed into *Outputs* using *Guides* to manage and control the process, and *Enablers* such as human resources, systems, data, and infrastructure to support execution of the process.

## *Inputs*

Inputs are provided by stakeholders and/or upstream business processes. They may be raw material, data, or any other thing that the process will transform into output. The inputs come from either some stakeholders, upstream business processes, or both. The input source may be internal or external to the Organization-in-Focus. An *Event* or a *Trigger* initiates the process at a certain time or within some time frame, for a specific reason - to deliver expected outputs with resulting outcomes through the execution of a relevant process.

Trigger Event = Time + Purpose + Expected Outputs/Resulting Outcomes

For example, when you order a book from an online book seller, the act of placing the order is the *event* which triggers or initiates the order fulfillment process. The input to this process might be the customer name, selected book information, and payment and shipment information. In process improvement initiatives, trigger events are also used to confirm the scope of the project boundaries and for validating the transformation flow. Similarly, in a manufacturing process, raw materials are converted into finished products. Irrespective of what raw material is being processed, it will carry its specification *data* as input and after the transformation, the data may become *information* about the transformed product. *Process* and *data* are dependent on one another. If process is a body, then data is the nervous system that enables all body functions. *Data* becomes information only when it interacts with a *process*. Consider the example of placing an order for a book: The data about the customer, book and payment amount becomes actionable information only after it is fed into the process.

## Outputs

Inputs are transformed by the process into outputs and outcomes. The outputs may be tangible things, while the outcomes may be the end result of a transaction. In our example of placing an order for a book, the output would be confirmation of the order and shipment of the book. But the outcome would be the customer's satisfaction with the overall experience of placing the order and receiving the book as requested. Outcomes are potential candidates for measures of success of a process and may become Key Performance Indicators. The data or the information that is the output of the process may become input or a guide to some downstream process such as the book inventory management process. The outputs may go to downstream business processes or stakeholders or both. The destination of the outputs could be internal or external to the Organization-in-Focus.

## Guides

Guides manage and control the transformation of inputs to their planned outputs. Unlike inputs, which are consumed or transformed by the process, guides are only referenced, not consumed. Guides may be provided by management business processes or stakeholders, both internal and/or external to the Organization-in-Focus. They can be classified into three categories:

- **Strategies and Governance**. Provide governance and guidelines to ensure that the day-to-day execution of the process-in-focus is aligned with organizational goals and objectives. The guidelines may include budget, measures of performance, and process ownership and managerial accountabilities.

- **Policy and Rules**. Business rules, practices, procedures, and compliance constraints that guide the execution of process steps with pre-established parameters for success and ensure mitigation of risk. These provide criteria for decision points within the process execution (the comprehensive discussion of business rules is outside the scope here). In an online book ordering process, the allowable customer credit limit and a customer's approval would be a business rule, while sales tax charges would be compliance control.

- **Information and Knowledge**. Knowledge includes internal and external information that may be used to optimize the success of the process based on past experiences. This also includes training materials for skills needed by the process performers who are the enablers of the process. In an online book ordering process, knowledge includes customer preferences and employee training material for handling the fulfill orders process.

The Guides are typically provided by the management processes of a business process blueprint, discussed in Chapter 3.

## Enablers

Enablers are the reusable resources of an organization that are engaged to support the process-in-focus. If the guides are sometimes referred to as the rules, the enablers are the tools. Enablers can be classified into three categories:

- **Human Capital (Organizational Roles)**. Roles represent the jobs or positions assigned to execute a process. This is the critical people-process link. The skills and competencies required to execute the process are used to define role profiles which, in turn, become job descriptions. Employees are assessed based on their performance measures aligned to these roles. To develop their capability, training of the employees is based on the competencies required by the processes. This is the human capital asset of an organization. This area is often referred to as "people training", but it must be understood that this is more comprehensive than just training. Defining Roles is an organizational design consideration and therefore needs the assistance of OD specialists (generally from within the Human Resources function).

- **Enabling Technology**. Technology is a broad term covering a variety of mechanisms that provide technical support to processes. This includes business application systems, data stores, IT tools and platforms, production lines, and general tools. For IT systems, SDLC is a professional practice and IT professionals are the resources who provide this enabler. Technology is a reusable asset.

- **Supporting Infrastructure**. The term Infrastructure covers a variety of platforms and foundations on which process enablers function. For people, Infrastructure includes work space, buildings, and energy. For systems, it includes hardware, software, and communications platforms. These are generally fixed assets.

These enablers are created by and sourced from their respective professional practice processes: Organizational roles are established by the professional practice of OD through organization design methodology. Application systems and databases are created by the professional practice of IT using Systems Development Life Cycle Methodology (SDLC). Likewise, various enabling mechanisms and the infrastructure would be created by their respective professional practices and methodologies. For example, the construction of a building would be made possible through engineering practices utilizing their relevant methodologies.

The Enablers are typically provided by the Support Processes of the business process blueprint discussed in Chapter 3.

## Key Points

- All processes, irrespective of industry and level in the hierarchy, have Inputs, Outputs, Guides, and Enablers. The inputs are consumed or transformed by a process into outputs and outcomes. Guides are referenced by the process and thus not consumed. Enablers are reusable resources of an organization.

- Processes are initiated by events. These events, also known as trigger events, initiate a process at a certain time or time frame and have a specific purpose with expected outputs and outcomes. In the redesign of processes, these trigger events are used for validating the workings of a process through scenarios representing each of the events.

- Inputs and guides come from either stakeholders, processes, or both, and Outputs go to some stakeholders, processes, or both. Enablers typically come from the processes of professional practices. These processes and stakeholders can be both internal and external to the process-in-focus.

- Guides are provided by the Management Processes of a Business Process Blueprint. The enablers are made available by the Support Processes of a Business Process Blueprint.

- All parts, objects, and resources have a specific place in the workings of a process. The "health" of the process is judged by the holistic workings of all parts of the process anatomy.

- If a process is the "body", data is the "nervous system" that enables all "body functions"—the process components.

- The Guides are the "rules" and enablers are the "tools"—the reusable resources of an organization.

Information about the processes is valuable knowledge which must be identified, captured, and made available for reuse. Some aspects of process knowledge may be represented by diagrams, text, pictures, icons, and even simulation scenarios. In other words, a process may be represented in one or more multimedia formats, depending on the objective and the audience. In this chapter, I will discuss the foundation of a process definition, which is needed in its most basic form of diagrams and text. Again, the levels of the process hierarchy imply the most appropriate representation of how work gets done at various levels of the organization. We will start with the scope diagram in Figure 5.1.

**Figure 5.1 Basic Process Scope diagram "Burlton IGOE"**

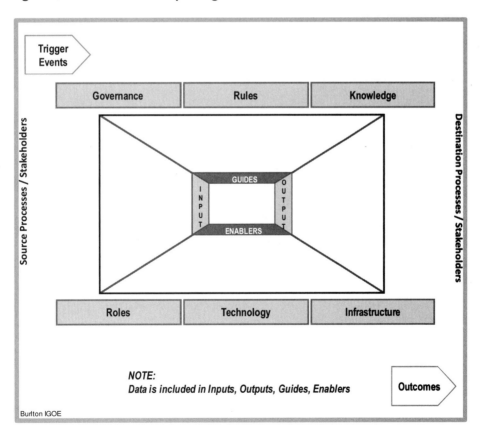

## *Process Components*

A basic process depiction is the central component of a *process structure* diagram. It is used to understand all parts of a process and to identify opportunities for improvement. The scope diagram template in Figure 5.1 is referred to as the Burlton IGOE (Inputs, Guides, Outputs and Enablers). It is one of the most comprehensive tools for understanding the workings of a process.

The components of process information include the following:

- **Trigger Events.** Process event triggers, the arrow on the upper left of Figure 5.1, represent unique triggers that initiate a process and have a specific purpose in terms of outputs and outcomes. A process may have multiple event triggers. For example, in an order fulfillment process for books, the triggers would include customer order, inquiry about a book, and checking of order status. In the process improvement activities, these triggers are used to run scenarios for validating the workings of a process.

- **IGOE Elements**. During the analysis of a business process, the IGOE process elements, inputs, guides, outputs and enablers, which surround the center box in Figure 5.1, are identified. The analysis should be conducted from the output side of a process first, in support of the concept that one should begin with the end in mind. If we examine a process from the input first, we run the risk of over-specifying inputs that are not needed to produce the output of finished products or a service.

- **Process Connections/Touch points**. Inputs and guides are sourced from business processes and/or stakeholders, the destinations of the outputs are business processes and/or stakeholders, and the enablers are sourced from professional practices. The analysis of the process yields an understanding of the touch points, from upstream to downstream. The process is a micro-view of the overall enterprise blueprint, and therefore the process touch points show the inter-dependencies among all processes in the Organization-in-Focus.

- **Data and Information**. Any data that are input to a process will be either consumed or transformed to output as information. Some data and information will be referenced as rules (guides), while others may be saved in data stores (enablers). Learning, in the form of information captured as outputs, may be used as inputs and guides by the same process itself. Data modeling is a technique for understanding the data needs of a process, and data models also facilitate identification of the data and business rules needed for decision support. They become the basis for designing data stores.

- **Knowledge Management**. There are many perspectives on knowledge management, but there is one simple, elegant answer for organizations that want to manage knowledge: design and capture knowledge in every mission critical process. Roger Burlton, a process leader, defines knowledge management this way: *Knowledge is learnings captured as output of the processes, used as inputs and guides; and embedded in enablers for sharing across the organization.* To accomplish this, make it a standard practice, on an ongoing basis, to identify what is being learned when a process is executing. Capture that information, store it in a document or database (enabler) so that process performers and managers can learn (guides) from that experience and make improvements.

## *Process Assessment*

For a business process to perform effectively and efficiently, all the elements of IGOE, including inputs, guides, outputs, enablers, the steps within the process, and the process interfaces, must work according to the desired specifications and expectations. A problem in any of these areas reduces the performance of the process. A periodic assessment, a "health check" of the process, may identify opportunities for improvement. As a result, a project for improving the process to remedy the shortcomings identified during the assessment could be initiated by the process owners and managers—as and when needed.

## *Professional Practices*

There are several professional disciplines that may be involved in the analysis, design, and improvement of business processes. Business process practitioners, which may include business analysts, process analysts, and technology analysts, need to work with an interdependent set of tools specific to the various components that comprise the business processes. An awareness of these disciplines is critical for managers who are assigned to improve the processes so that they may marshal the right tools from the right practices. These professional disciplines include: Strategic Planning, which drives the mission of the process and thus acts as a guide; Performance Management, which defines and monitors measurements; BPM or Business Process Management, the overall practice of managing the process assets of an organization; OD or Organization Development & Design, the practice of aligning people resources to the process and facilitating Human Change; IT, the practice of creating systems; and other infrastructure related practices. Last, but not least, the overarching practice of Program and Project Management is fundamental to managing the business process assets.

## *Process Documentation*

Information about processes should be documented so that it can be used for communication and to promote reusability of this asset by process stakeholders and project teams who may conduct analysis for improvements. Each business process should have a unique identifier and a definition. The definition may be textual and graphic or diagrammatic. The diagrammatic concepts and guidelines for defining a process will be covered in the next chapter.

There are two ways to identify a process (and its sub-processes) – by its unique *name* and/or its unique *identifier*. A good naming convention, along with an agreed definition, makes communication among business workers and managers easier and promotes a consistent, common language throughout the organization.

A process name should be in Noun – Verb form, with the purpose of the process implicit in its name—to the extent possible. The name must be unique within the organization with a name format of: From Triggering Event (an active verb) to Target Outcome (noun). For example, **Recruit** (action) and **Hire Employees** (outcome) process

Some other examples are: **Order to Cash** process, **Procure to Pay** process, and **Market to Customer** process. Gerunds, verbal nouns, ending in "ing", should be avoided (example: accounting, manufacturing). The names must be suffixed by the term "process" to ensure that this organizational artifact is differentiated from others, such as functions, roles, and systems. Some verbs, such as *manage*, *maintain*, and *handle*, should be avoided as much as possible because they are a little too general and make the purpose of the process obscure (also the verb *process* for a process name should be avoided). Sometimes, of course, at enterprise levels 1 and 2 especially, these terms may be unavoidable due to lack of awareness on the part of business managers in conforming to appropriate naming convention.

Identifiers must be unique across the organization. They should be standardized within the organization for consistency and for facilitating storage in process repository software. The identifiers are used for reference only and should not imply sequence or priority. In Figure 5.2, the identifiers are standardized hierarchically.

**Figure 5.2 NewAge Foods Process Documentation**

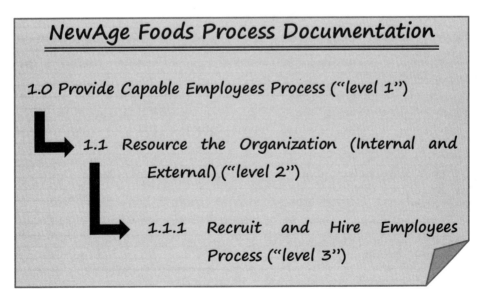

The 1.0 **Provide Capable Employees** process is an enterprise process at Level 1, the sub-process 1.1 **Resource the Organization** is a Level 2 process in this context, and 1.1.1 **Recruit and Hire Employees** process would be a Level 3 process.

## *Process Definition*

The following template in Table 5.1 is a list of attributes that may be documented for business processes definitions. Some of these attributes may not be necessary, or relevant, for all processes at different levels of detail in the process hierarchy. However, a minimum set of these attributes should be agreed on as a standard requirement in an organization. The definition should include information needed by the process performers and managers for decision making and controls when executing the process; and technology analysts should have technical information for developing and maintaining data, systems, and underlying support infrastructure. In Table 5.1, an example of NewAge Foods **Recruit and Hire Employees** process shows the type of information needs to be considered for documenting business process knowledge. This example is not intended to be a complete solution, but rather a sketch of what the content could look like. The items of the process documentation are in the order of importance to the NewAge organization.

**Table 5.1 NewAge Foods Recruit and Hire Employees Process Documentation**

| Process Name (verb-noun): | Recruit and Hire Employees process |
|---|---|
| Process Unique Identifier: | 20.1 (assuming that this is a "child" of the parent process 20.0 in the process architecture of NewAge Foods) |
| Process Context (name of the parent or super-process): | 20.0 Provide Capable Employees Process |
| Version Control (date, identifier, author): | Version 1.1, DDMMMYYYY, Artie Mahal |

| Business Process Owner/Manager: | Director of Human Resources |
|---|---|
| Purpose: | The purpose of the process is to recruit and hire employees for the North American snacks business, including office and sales staff. |
| Summary: | The Human Capital Strategy of the organization states "Attract, retain, and motivate highly engaged, diverse employees."<br><br>In alignment with this strategy, the HR staffing team hires competent employees through this process to fulfil the talent pipeline of the organization. This process includes internal and external candidates for open positions. Recruitment is done through the corporate website, universities, referrals, and job placement entities. The sourcing also includes the local community, to promote good will. Hiring is done through a merit based approach with a competent selection of interview panels. Candidates and other stakeholders involved in the process are kept informed on a timely basis—on agreed service levels. |
| Event Triggers & Frequency: | Annual Human Capital Planning Calendar<br><br>Open positions – as needed<br><br>Transfers, Separations, and Retirements<br><br>Mergers and Acquisitions – as needed |
| Timing Constraints: | Each candidate must be processed from the time of application to decision point within 4 weeks. |
| Best Practice Statements: | Human Resource industry practices will be utilized, as appropriate. For example, the workforce demographics of the changing needs are utilized. Example: Generation "Millennium" may have different needs for their work environment than Generation "X". |

| Performance Measures/KPI's: | See Figure 12.4 in Chapter 12. |
|---|---|
| **Process Critical Compliance Factors:** | Compliance with the state and federal guideline of equal employment, and adherence to corporate policies and procedures. |
| **Outputs:** | Sample Outputs:<br>• Hired Employees<br>• Contract<br>• Rejected Candidates/Notice Letters |
| **Inputs:** | Sample Inputs:<br>• Existing Employees/Candidates<br>• External Candidates<br>• Candidate Referrals |
| **Process Models:** | These models would be documented here:<br>Process Scope Diagram and<br>Process Flow Diagram (see Figure 12.10 in Chapter 12) |
| **Data Model:** | At the minimum, identify Fundamental Data Entities and Data Rules here.<br>See Conceptual Model Figure 12.21 in Chapter 12 |
| **Business Rules:** | Sample Business Rules:<br>Internal candidates must have the approval of their current manager before applying for a position.<br><br>Employees who take on a new position cannot apply for another position for a period of 6 months. |

| Guides (Governance, Rules, Knowledge): | Sample Guides:<br>• Governance<br>• Talent Acquisition Plan<br>• Budget<br>• Rules<br>• Job Specifications<br>• Employment laws<br>• Knowledge<br>• Interview tools<br>• Benchmarks and trends |
|---|---|
| Enablers (Organizational Roles, Technology, Infrastructure): | Sample Enablers:<br>• Roles<br>• Hiring manager<br>• Candidate<br>• Technology<br>• Corporate Website<br>• HR System<br>• Infrastructure<br>• Interview Facility<br>• Ad Agency Network |
| Changes History: | This process was changed from Version 1.0 on DDMMMYYY to update the recruitment cycle time from 8 weeks to 4 weeks. |
| Process Improvement Plan: | There needs to be more effort on sourcing candidates from the local communities, per the strategy. The corporate public relations group will be consulted to find a better solution to meet that objective. This is targeted for first quarter of the year. |

## *Process Repository*

If you view processes as an asset, then it follows that all knowledge about this asset should be planned, created, stored, maintained, and reused to optimize the operation of an organization. There are a multitude of tools that may be employed in the creation and documentation of this knowledge asset. The documentation may take a variety of forms, including (but not limited to) text, diagrams, and videos.

A process repository is an effective way to capture and share knowledge across the organization. There are passive and active software repositories in the evolving market place. Passive repositories are tools that store the information in electronic form, but may not have file sharing capabilities and lack the ability to coordinate simultaneous updates of information by multiple users. The active repositories can accommodate multiple views of process information, provide a way to record and retrieve what-uses impact analysis, and may be shared among users who are geographically dispersed.

There are several repositories in this space. See Chapter 11 for some more detail on the classification of various tools. Obviously, a passive solution is less expensive than an active solution. It is advisable, therefore, to experiment with less expensive solutions in the beginning, and to establish standards and practices for building and documenting process knowledge before making a large, strategic investment. The discussion of specific software tools is outside the scope of this book.

## *Process Knowledge Example*

The simple example in Figure 5.3 of the **Bake-a-Cake** process shows how the process components may be identified for understanding and analyzing a process.

**Figure 5.3 Process Scope Diagram Example (Bake-a-Cake Process)**

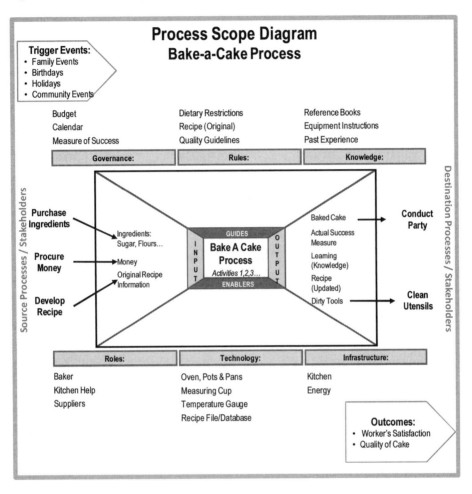

The **Bake-a-Cake** process is initiated by one of these events: family events, birthdays, holidays, or community events. These events occur at certain timeframes and trigger baking a cake. For execution of the process, certain guides and enablers must be in place:

- **Guides**. Governance includes the budget, committed time frame, and measures of success of the process. Rules include the recipe and quality guidelines. And Knowledge includes past experience with baking and any instructions needed to use the equipment.
- **Enablers**. Roles include baker and kitchen help. Technology includes oven, pots and pans as "mechanisms". The recipe file is data/information to be used by the process. And the kitchen

and electric or gas energy is the Infrastructure. The input ingredients will be obtained through the **Purchase Ingredients** process, money through the **Procure Money** process, and the recipe from the **Develop Recipe** process. The **Bake-a-Cake** process, itself, has steps that execute according to a specified sequence. These steps are the activities, tasks, and work instructions depicting a process hierarchy. The output, a baked cake, becomes input to a destination process, **Conduct Party** process, and dirty utensils go to the **Clean Utensils** process. The Outcome of work satisfaction relates to the role of the baker and helper, and the quality of the cake relates to the compliance specifications of the recipe. The structure of every process is the same as the **Bake-a-Cake** process. This process knowledge becomes the baseline for further analysis to troubleshoot and improve the process for optimal performance.

## Insights

Process Scope Analysis should be a standard practice in all organizations. It not only allows the examination of a given process in its own right, but it also facilitates the identification of upstream and downstream process touch points, thus promoting the value of an organizational business process blueprint (architecture).

In Physiology, homeostasis is the ability of a living organism to adjust its internal environment to create equilibrium and balance: "...property of a system, either open or closed, that regulates its internal environment and tends to maintain a stable, constant condition...typically used to refer to a living organism."[1] While business process cannot self regulate its balance without external intervention (except perhaps some highly technical aspects, such as in robotics), the Process Scope Diagram and its knowledge is a comprehensive tool for assessing process health and for correcting

---

[1] Wikipedia

imbalances within its workings (I refer to this as *"Process-Homeostasis"*).

This tool and its supporting techniques should be a standard in all organizations, irrespective of whether they use *Redesign, Lean or Six Sigma* techniques for process improvement and redesign. Redesign is a method for innovating a process, Lean is a technique to remove waste from the process, and Six Sigma is a technique for eliminating defects in products or services. All three methods and techniques fall under the umbrella of BPM. Kiran Garimella in his book *The Power of Process* states: "Lean takes the fat out of the process, and BPM keeps it out!"

## Key Points

- Business processes knowledge includes process definitions and their detailed attributes. In addition to text, the definitions may include graphic diagrams, pictures, and videos. The content of process definitions should be standardized to ensure compliance and consistency of use across the organization. Standards are important for compliance and automation, but common sense is also critical to deciding what really is important for the organization to adopt.

- Documentation of what has been learned about a process is reusable, thus reducing the cost of repeatedly analyzing and generating the same definitions across multiple business areas. It also promotes a common language for effectiveness and efficiency among workers and the projects they work on. "Money not spent is money earned".

- Business Process Knowledge Repositories are either passive or active. Passive repositories have limitations, but they are a good way to learn and establish standards and practices before investing in an active repository. Active process repositories require dedicated resources and, therefore, require ROI justification by management. The benefits of the reusability of knowledge, while easy to understand intellectually, are much harder to achieve without the absolute commitment of management in providing funding and holding process owners accountable.

Models, or "Maps", are a visual representation of patterns and their meaning that facilitate understanding and communication about topics of interest. They simplify complexity by using diagrams, pictures, scenarios, simulation patterns, and icons that are relevant to the subject at hand for their intended audience. In this chapter, I will show process and data modeling practices and standards that may be used by process performers, managers, and analysts to define how their work gets done. While IT analysts and technicians should understand this language to effectively translate it into technical specifications, technical models are out of the scope of this book.

## *Process Models*

As we discussed in an earlier chapter, business process is a hierarchy whose levels we will refer to as Levels 0, 1, 2, 3, 4, and 5+. While some standards for documentation, such as Flowcharting, have been used for decades, recently enhanced standards such as Business Process Modeling Notation (BPMN), also known as "swimlanes", is relatively new. Then there are standards for specific process improvement methodologies, such as Lean. The most appropriate modeling convention(s) chosen from among many options may differ for each process level in the hierarchy.

### LEVEL 1

There are three variations of processes at this level: First, the Business Process Blueprint (Architecture), second, an individual process within the architecture, and third, a value chain encompassing multiple processes. The template in Figure 6.1 is a guide for the layout of the process blueprint.

**Figure 6.1 Business Process Blueprint Template**

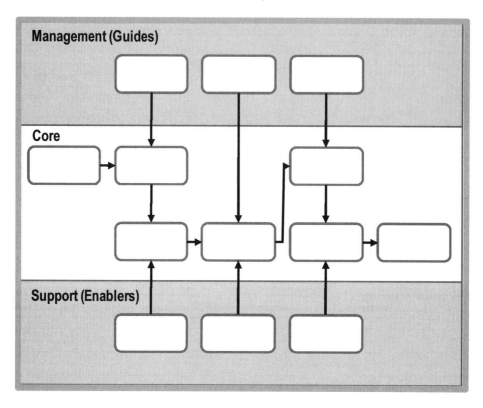

To document a Business Process Blueprint (Architecture), start with the set of Core processes (those that produce and deliver products and services as outputs and achieve the strategic intent of the organization, such as **Market-to-Customer**) in the center; Management processes (those which govern the organization, such as **Develop Strategic Plans**) at the top, and Support processes (those processes that provide resources to the Core processes for their operation such as **Provide Capable Employees**) at the bottom of the diagram. At this macro-level, process input and output flows may be kept to a minimum to avoid cluttering the diagram.

One practical approach is to show the process flow summary outputs and inputs only for the Core processes. Figure 6.2 is an example of a business process blueprint for the NewAge Foods Company. In this diagram, there are two value chains, one for the customer (Products Value Chain), and the other for the consumer (Service Value Chain). Customers include wholesalers and retailers, whereas consumers are the individuals buying products directly from the manufacturer through their mail order side of the business. A technique that is sometimes used for ease of communicating is to show the value chains in different colors to differentiate them. A noteworthy aspect in this map is an example of processes shared by two value chains: **Secure Manufacturing Capacity**.

### Figure 6.2 Business Process Architecture / Blueprint

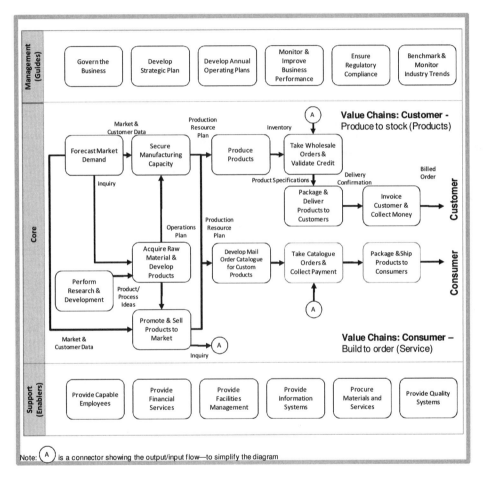

Each of the business processes at this level should have a Process Scope Diagram using the IGOE structure that uses the template in Figure 6.3, which was discussed in the previous chapter (recall Figure 5.1). The Process Scope Diagram becomes a comprehensive specification of a business process along with its touch points to other processes. An example of a Process Scope Diagram from the NewAge Foods Process Architecture is shown in Figure 6.4.

**Figure 6.3 Business Process Scope Diagram – IGOE Template**

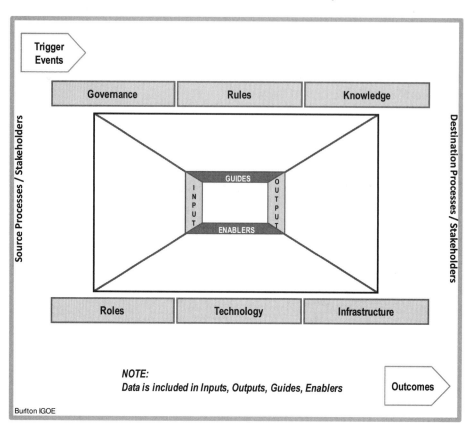

**NewAge Foods Process Scope Diagram**

When the support process **Provide Capable Employees** from Figure 6.2 is detailed into its lower level processes, one process, **Recruit and Hire Employees** process, will have the Process Scope Diagram shown in Figure 6.4. More details on this diagram are covered in Chapter 12.

**Figure 6.4 Process Scope Diagram Example**

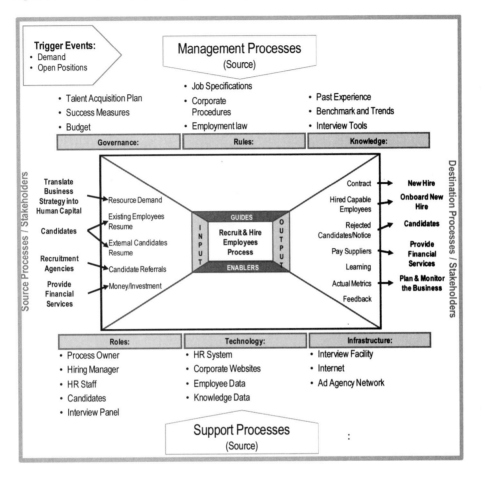

## LEVEL 2

This is the next finer level of detail from a Level 1 process and may contain five to nine sub-processes—the rule of 7 +/- 2. It is documented as a *Lateral Flow Diagram* and may show the guides and enablers for each of the sub-processes. A Lateral Flow Diagram, shown in Figure 6.5, is simply a sequential way of documenting processes. The notation on either end of the process flow diagram in Figure 6.3 shows the start and end of the process. These two notations are part of the BPMN diagramming standard, which will be discussed next.

As in Level 1, each of the sub-processes at this level would have its own process flow diagram using the IGOE structure.

**Figure 6.5 Level 2 Process Flow Diagram**

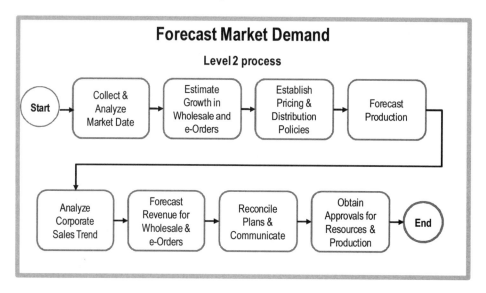

## LEVELS 3 & 4

Level 3 is a further decomposition of the sub-processes from Level 2. Each of the Level 2 sub-processes may be decomposed into 7 +/2 sub-processes, known as Activities. This is the level of detail where the "rubber meets the road", so to speak. At this level, procedures may be synthesized for documenting who does what, how, where, and when. It is the basis for creating organization design, managing human change, training process performers, and designing business transactional applications. Depending on the level of analysis needed, one or more of the Level 3 activities may be either documented in detail using BPMN standards or as a lateral flow diagram, as shown in the Level 2 section.

When using the Lean method, a unique diagram known as *Value Stream Mapping* is documented (see Figure 6.7). Irrespective of the methods used, a Process Scope Diagram using IGOE template must be created prior to detailing out a Level 3 diagram. The Level 3 Activity detailed steps become Level 4 sub-processes, known as *Tasks*. Examples of these diagramming conventions will be shown later in the chapter.

## *Business Process Modeling Notation (BPMN)*

The BPMN standard was formalized in 2004 by the Object Management Group (OMG). This method of depicting a process flow is not new; it has been known by many names, such as deployment chart, Rumbler-Brache diagram, and now, simply a Swimlane model. This is one of the most useful models for understanding and analyzing how work is performed in detail. The structure of this convention is shown in Figure 6.6 (partial notations shown).

**Figure 6.6 Swimlane: Process Flow Diagram Format**

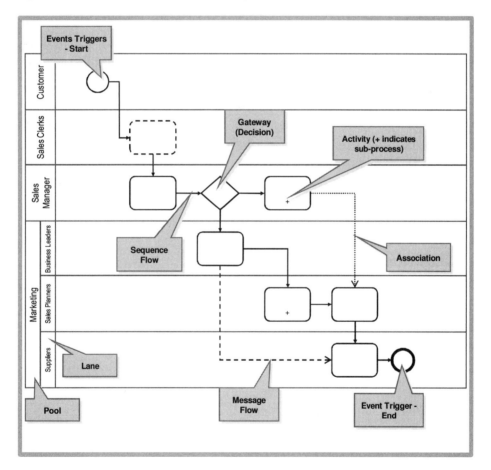

The customer is documented at the top of the model and suppliers at the bottom. The processes performers' roles are on the left, documented in top-down order of how they connect with the customer. The process flow is documented in left-right and top-down order. The left to right flow depicts cycle time. The inputs and outputs are shown using different flow notations, such as material flow and information flow.

The BPMN diagram is intended for business people and both process and technical analysts. However, for technical analysts, the standard offers more rigor, designed to automate processes for workflow software and Business Process Management System (BPMS). The technical aspect is out of scope in this book. However, for business process performers, managers, and analysts, the main consideration in using this standard is to provide clarity in how work is getting done, who is doing it, and when.

While this standard provides a variety of icons, common sense must be applied to ensure the model is not overly complicated. For example, it is better to use only one symbol for process outputs and for information flow by simply documenting the nature of the flow on the flow notation itself, rather than multiple flows among the same two processes. A common question is, "How do we know we need to create a Swimlane versus a lateral flow diagram?" The "5-7 rule" is very helpful here: If there are five or more organizational roles involved in the process, then it is a candidate for a Swimlane model.

### Lean – Value Stream Mapping

Lean comes from the concept that processes should be lean. That is, without any non value added steps. Value stream mapping is a Lean manufacturing technique used to analyze the flow of materials and information to bring a product or service to a consumer. At Toyota, where the technique originated, it is known as "material and information flow mapping". The icons and symbols of this convention fall into three categories: *Material Flow*, *Information Flow*, and *General Icons*.

In Figure 6.7, an example value stream map shows the logistics transfer of manufactured products from the factory to the warehouses, to the transfer points, and finally to the retail stores. All along this journey, data is collected and analyzed to seek opportunities for making the process Lean. While Lean methodology does not call for an overall process scope diagram showing process touch points through a well defined architecture, it is strongly recommend that an IGOE - Process Scope Diagram be standardized in organizations using Lean, prior to detailing a value stream map. Lean is a technique within the overall BPM practice.

**Figure 6.7 Value Stream Map (Lean) Example**

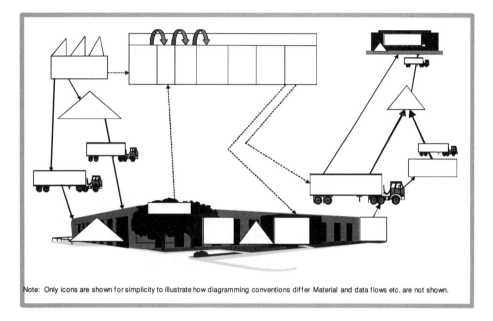

Note: Only icons are shown for simplicity to illustrate how diagramming conventions differ Material and data flows etc. are not shown.

## LEVEL 5

Level 3 Activities and Level 4 Tasks are further decomposed into Level 5 or lower Work Instructions. At this lower level of detail, there are generally one or two process performer roles involved, but there may be numerous data and business rules utilized. The appropriate method for documenting the work instructions is Flowcharting, accompanied by textual details.

A *flowchart* is a commonly used diagram that represents an algorithm or process by showing the steps as boxes of various kinds, and their order by connecting them with arrows. Flowcharts are used in analyzing, designing, documenting or managing a process or program in various fields. Flowcharting uses a variety of symbols to communicate flow. The symbols include process, document, inputs/outputs, decision, and connectors. The example in Figure 6.8 is of a flow chart showing some of the symbols. Most of the time, it is unnecessary to decompose processes lower than Level 5, except in some isolated cases. It is important to evaluate why you think it is necessary to go lower than this level before going down that path.

**Figure 6.8 Flowchart Example**

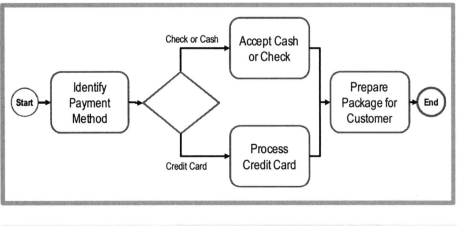

## *Process Story*

Business processes are simply a business story: who does what, how, when, and where. And where does this story start and where does it end? Any change or improvement to processes should be communicated effectively to all relevant stakeholders. A creative way to do this is the use of a metaphor and an accompanying diagram which tells the story in a very simple and understandable format. Acceptance of formal processes by the audience will be easier when preceded by a metaphorical story. Of course, there are other methods for telling the process story, such as storyboarding, simulation, and even verbal narration when presenting a process model in person. Figure 6.9 is an example of a story of product conversion from raw material (peanuts) to finished product (snack bar)—farm to factory processes of the NewAge Foods Company.

**Figure 6.9 Business Process "Story"**

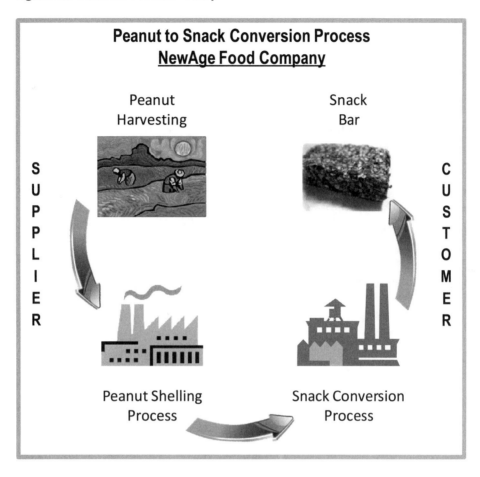

## Data Models

Data may be defined as facts needed to execute process and to understand work done. These facts are input to a process and then, through its execution, are consumed or transformed into information. Data only becomes information when it is transformed through some process to achieve specific outputs. Process and data are co-dependent - one without the other has little value. If process is the "body", data is the "nervous system" that flows through it. For example, if you order a book online, you provide data facts as input on a website, which in turn triggers the order fulfillment process of the supplier. As we saw in the Anatomy of a Process, data input becomes output information. When lessons learned information is captured as one of the outputs, it becomes knowledge to be used next time around as a process guide. Data and information are stored in data stores as enablers for sharing knowledge and supporting business application systems.

Similar to process modeling, data modeling has its own discipline, modeling conventions, and terminology. Data models help identify data needs and business rules for getting work done, and thus support the execution and governance of processes. There are three types of data models: *conceptual data models*, *logical data models,* and *physical data models*. Each of these depicts data facts in a structure known as an Entity Relationship Diagram or ER Diagram, as shown in Figure 6.10.

**Figure 6.10 Conceptual Data Model Example**

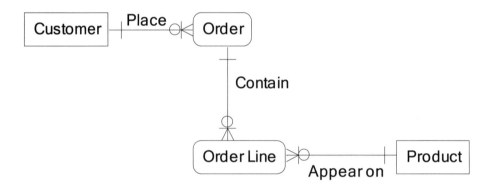

An online book store would need to know information about their customers and would, therefore, have a customer data store, whereas a corner gas station may not have the need, will, or means to store customer information and, therefore, will not have a customer data store. The characteristics of each of the data entities are described by their *attributes*. For example, the data attributes of a Customer entity might include Customer Identifier, Customer Name, Customer Address, and Customer Telephone Number. And for an Employee data entity, the attributes might include Employee Identifier, Employee Name, Employee Address, and Employee Data of Birth. Data entities may be related to other data entities for a business reason. For example, a Customer places an Order for a Product on a certain Date (Customer, Order, Product, and Time are data entities). The relationships among these entities define business facts and help identify business rules and decision points for control and execution of processes. See Figure 6.11 for the NewAge Foods Business Rules.

**Figure 6.11 NewAge Foods Business Rules**

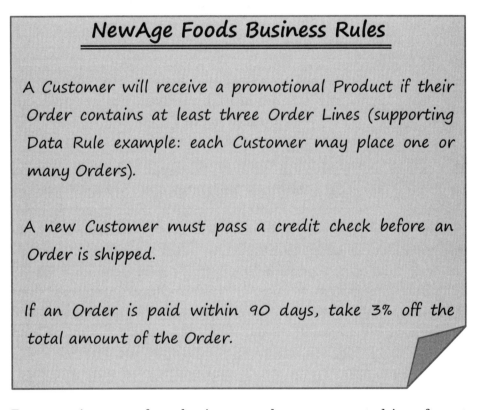

Data requirements for a business need are represented in a format known as meta-data, or data about data, that is the basis for defining data models and structures. The basic component of a data model is a *data entity*, which is defined by Bill Smith, a data discipline pioneer as: *A person, place, concept, event or a thing about which a company has the need, will and means to store information. As a standard, data entities are named with a singular noun.* For example, Customer, Employee, and Product are data entities. Table 6.1 has the definition of three major components that make up a basic data model.

**Table 6.1 Entity Relationship Definitions**

| | |
|---|---|
| **Entity** | Is a set of data about a person, place, concept, thing or event needed by the business to perform their functions and execute processes. For example, Customer, Product, and Employee. |
| **Attribute** | Is a basic data element which belongs to, and describes, an entity. For example, Customer Name, Product Number, and Employee Name. |
| **Relationship** | Shows an association between two entities and the number of each involved. For example, one Customer places many Orders, and one Order is for one Customer. |

The data model provides a common language among the process performers, managers, business analysts, data analysts, process analysts, and technology analysts to have a meaningful dialogue around the information requirements of getting work done. Using this as communication tool, business requirements that include business rules and functional requirements are identified for an application. Progressive versions of data models are developed from the beginning of a business need to the creation of databases and applications. Conceptual models facilitate business context and policies support, logical models facilitate data and business rules support, and physical data models provide the data store structures to support business functions and application systems.

## CONCEPTUAL DATA MODEL

A *conceptual data model* is a set of data models at a high level of abstraction, comparable to the Business Process Blueprint. At this level, a model presents the categories or subject areas of data and information that are needed to operate the enterprise. The conceptual data model is roughly comparable to business process Levels 0, 1, and 2. Conceptual data models are high-level concepts that aid in understanding and simplifying the complexity of an Organization-in-Focus. Some common subject areas are Customer, Product, Employee, and Organization.

## LOGICAL DATA MODEL

A *logical data model* is an expansion of one or more conceptual data model subject areas to a lower level of detail. For example, if the conceptual data model has a Customer subject area, the logical data model will provide the specific information about a customer that the business is interested in keeping. A logical data model is used to understand and analyze the business information needs and underlying data and business rules. Process performers and managers supported by analysts can use the logical data models to understand and shape their needs for information and subsequent systems application. Here the entities and relationships are expanded and attributes are identified. The logical data model is roughly comparable to business process Levels 2, 3, and 4. This tool should be used by the business to communicate their data needs, facilitated by the business, process, and systems analysts appropriate to the need. These models facilitate technical specifications for applications data needs.

## PHYSICAL DATA MODEL

The logical data model is handed over to the systems analysts for application design, and a database designer (Data Base Administrator or DBA for short) who converts the entities into tables, attributes into data elements or fields, and the relationships into navigation paths in a relational database. Most packaged software has these structures embedded in their ready-to-use applications. In the context of business processes, these tables and elements may be constructed from Level 5 and below.

These models facilitate the creation of technical solutions for data and information access, usage, and storage.

### Process and Data Modeling Matrix

Note: Wherever process models are created, as shown in Table 6.2, they must be accompanied by their textual descriptions. Creation of text by itself is not identified in the table, in all cases.

**Table 6.2 Guide for Modeling Conventions/Insights**

| Process Level | Model Purpose | Business Purpose | Process Models | Data Models |
|---|---|---|---|---|
| Level 0 | Value Proposition | Enterprise Value Chain to measure and manage enterprise performance | Enterprise Context Diagram<br><br>Level 1 Processes summarized under a defined Value Chain<br><br>List of Fundamental Data Entities | Enterprise Conceptual Data Model and Subject Areas |
| Level 1 | Business Process Architecture/ Blueprint | Business Intent and Strategy to set organizational direction<br><br>Business Unit/Divisional Performance Management | Level 1 Processes organized in Management – Core – Support structure<br><br>Process Scope Diagrams (IGOE) for each Level 1 Process | Conceptual Data Model for Process-in-Focus<br><br>List of Fundamental Data Entities for Process-in-Focus |
| Level 2 | Blueprint Level 1 Sub-processes | Business Policies to define ways of operating<br><br>Functional Performance Management | Level 2 Processes organized in Lateral Flow Diagrams<br><br>Process Scope Diagram (IGOE) for each Level 2 process<br><br>Includes Process Flow Diagram (BPMN/Swimlanes) may be appropriate | Conceptual/Logical Data Model for Process-in-Focus<br><br>Includes Fundamental Data Entities, Relationships and Key Attributes |

| Process Level | Model Purpose | Business Purpose | Process Models | Data Models |
|---|---|---|---|---|
| Level 3-4 | Activities and Tasks | Process Activities, Business Rules, Decision Points, and Procedures | Level 3 Processes to be documented as Process Scope Diagram (IGOE) <br><br> Includes Lateral Flow Diagram or Process Flow Diagram (BPMN/Swimlane) | Logical Data Model for Process-in-Focus <br><br> Includes Fundamental Data Entities, Relationships, Key Attributes, all Attributes, and Data Rules |
| Level 5+ | Tasks and Work Instructions | Standard Operating Procedures <br><br> Business Rules: <br><br> Detailed Steps for Working and Automation | Flowcharting; Textual Descriptions | Initiation of Physical Data Models for Process-in-Focus <br><br> Includes Tables, Data Types, Data Element/Fields, Columns, Indexes |

## Use of Standards

A picture is worth thousand words! While that wisdom is essential in process and data modeling, there is an additional consideration: the right picture, at the right level of detail, for the right audience! For business process modeling, BPMN is one of the common standards that address the needs of business process performers and managers, and business analysts. However, you should be careful when deciding to what extent you want to use all aspects of this standard. As always, common sense helps keeps things practical and simple. On a separate note, a new standard, Business Entity Definitions Language (BEDL) is being developed by IBM to possibly complement process and data considerations in relation to the life cycle of business entities. As it matures, this may further promote the need for data models as a proactive artifact, rather than being an afterthought in process analysis.

Some business process improvement techniques, such as Six Sigma, Lean, and Process Redesign, need the use of Process Scope Diagram (IGOE) as a standard, preceding their individual and preferred modeling notations. The practitioners of these methods seem to continue playing in their own sandboxes, rather than collaborating and showing "one face" to the customer—the business organizations—by aligning the use of these complimentary tools under one BPM umbrella. Most recently, it has becoming popular to combine Lean and Six Sigma and refer to it as the Lean Six Sigma method. In any case, this confusion continues. While we wait for the industry gurus of these disciplines to arrive at a common agreement, the process professionals should at least standardize on the use of the Process Scope Diagram (Burlton, IGOE).

Development of data models has been a standard practice in the data processing discipline now known as Information Technology. When packaged software started to become popular, data models were integrated into the physical structures of the design. Software companies promised that data models would be incorporated into their packages to improve flexibility - they have accomplished that. But, the models underlying the software are the physical data models. The conceptual and logical data models, which use the terminology of the business users, process performers, managers, and business analysts, are only represented in application screen layouts. Process and data are inseparable. Therefore, Business Process Management professionals must make conceptual and logical data models an integral part of the process design toolkit to enhance the quality of analysis.

## Key Points

- Models or "Maps" are a graphic format supported by textual descriptions and narratives that tell a business story. Models are most effective when they are targeted to the right audience and are presented at the right level of detail. A picture is worth a thousand words...only if it is at the right level of detail and tells the right business story to the right audience!

- Process models have a hierarchy which determines the type of models most appropriate at each level of representation. The content of models is process knowledge, and thus, a reusable asset.

- Processes and data are co-dependent - one has little purpose without the other. Therefore, a process model should have a corresponding data model. The process model tells the story of how work gets done and the data model depicts the facts and rules needed to successfully execute a process.

- Both process and data models promote an understanding of how an organization works and what information it needs. These are effective tools for promoting dialogue among process performers, managers, executives, business analysts, process analysts, and technology analysts to develop business and application solutions.

Nature has experimented, evolving life and matter since the beginning of time. One of the most efficient two-dimensional patterns or models in nature is the hexagon—the six-sided graphic model used by many forms of life and matter. See Figure 7.1.

**Figure 7.1 Process Configuration Model "Burlton Hexagon"**

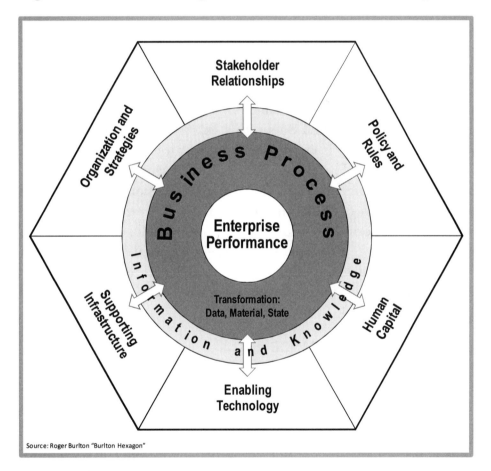

Source: Roger Burlton "Burlton Hexagon"

The hexagon can accommodate seven equal and concentric circles to fill the space within its boundaries. We see these patterns in snow flakes, honey bee hives, and even patterns formed by gases on one of the planets in the universe. According to neural biology, humans use a technique called configurable processing, piecing together the components to form recognizable patterns. For example, by looking at eyes, ears, and nose, a human differentiates one face from another. For business processes, the natural pattern of the hexagon in Figure 7.1 describes parts which, when synchronized well, would provide optimal performance. I refer to that pattern as the Process Configuration Model. This model was developed by Roger Burlton and is also known as the "Burlton Hexagon".

## Process Configuration Model Explanation

Enterprise performance is delivered through the execution of one or more business processes in an organization. A process may be simply defined as "how work gets done". Business processes have two sets of elements that support execution: the guide elements, which are Organization and Strategies, Stakeholder Relationships, and Policies and Rules; and Enable elements, which are Human Capital, Enabling Technology, and Supporting Infrastructure. Information is used and Knowledge is created throughout all of these elements via relevant Business Processes. Business Processes and their guides and enablers are critical assets of an organization which must be understood, aligned, and optimized to ensure delivery of desired and sustainable performance. This comprehensive model also provides an understanding of the professional practices that are directly or indirectly utilized to synchronize all elements for effectiveness and efficiency. The following outline provides an overview of the Process Configuration Model (PCM).

### ENTERPRISE PERFORMANCE

We start in the center of the model in Figure 7.1 with enterprise performance. Enterprise performance may be described as a set of measurable goals and objectives necessary for the viability and success of an organizational entity. The organization is expected to deliver some predefined value to its customers and stakeholders, both internal and external to the organization. When aligned with business processes and other relevant aspects of the business, Key Performance Indicators (KPI) provide the mechanism for measuring performance. Any gap in performance, or a reason to enhance their capabilities, causes examination of the processes, their guides, enablers, and information usage. The professional discipline utilized here is: Business Performance Management.

## BUSINESS PROCESSES

Enveloped around enterprise performance are the business processes, implying that all work done to deliver performance takes place through the execution of one or more business processes. Triggered by a business event, the business processes take inputs from one or more source processes or supplier-stakeholders and transform them into the desired outputs and outcomes. The outputs are then passed to destination processes and/or customer-stakeholders. Typically *Data*, *Material*, and *State* of things or concepts are transformed via the processes. An example of state would be a customer order transformed into a fulfilled order after completion of the transaction of delivery of products or services via the execution of sales logistics processes. The professional practices engaged in the improvement of the process include: the overall discipline of Business Process Management (BPM) and its supporting methods, such as Process Improvement, Redesign and Lean Six Sigma.

## INFORMATION AND KNOWLEDGE

Information and knowledge surround the processes in the diagram and connect to each of the elements of the guides and enablers through a two-way exchange. Data is a critical resource of an organization and is pervasive throughout all elements of the business process and its configuration. When processed for an event, the data is transformed into information by the execution of the business processes, resulting in some business knowledge. And the application of that knowledge creates solutions that may be considered the resulting "wisdom" or business acumen. While the information resides in data stores and is used and updated by the processes, the knowledge is utilized as process guides for effectiveness, compliance, and innovation. As stated earlier in the book, if process is the "body", information is the "nervous system" that makes the "anatomy", the organization, function. The supporting professional practices include: Data Management and Knowledge Management.

## GUIDES

Guides provide governance, stakeholder expectations, direction, funding, policies, rules, and compliance constraints to business processes through the application of information and knowledge. These are the three elements in the upper part of the Process Configuration Model:

- **Organization and Strategies**. Organization and Strategies constitute organizational governance and its support structure. The word "governance" derives from a Greek verb that means to *steer*. Governance in that context relates to consistent management, cohesive policies, processes, and decision-rights for a given area of responsibility. The support structure to carry out governance includes organization design, which includes the alignment of people and processes to achieve vision and deliver results. The strategies then, through programs and projects, execute processes for delivering the desired performance. In the context of the process, this guide in the model refers to the organization and strategies impacting process-in-scope. Professional practices include Strategic Planning, Organization Development (OD) - which includes Organization Design, and Program and Project Management.

- **Stakeholder Relationships**. The Stakeholder Relationships relate to identifying stakeholders, understanding their expectations, nurturing their trust, and promoting mutual loyalty to ensure the organization's success through the delivery of the promised value proposition. The stakeholders may be defined as the individuals and organizational entities who have a vested interest in the success of the organization and are the beneficiaries of its performance. The stakeholders include owners, customers, suppliers, employees, regulatory agencies, communities, and even competitors, in some cases. In the context of the process, this guide in the model refers to the stakeholders for process-in-scope. Professional practices include Stakeholders Relationship Management.

- **Policies and Rules**. Shaped by the strategic intent of an organization and direction provided by its governance, business policies and rules are established to ensure compliance and mitigate risk through appropriate controls, checks, and balances. These policies provide the business decision-making framework at all levels of the organization, and are implemented through standard operating procedures that provide controls to the execution of business processes. The supporting professional practices here include Business Rules Management and Risk Management.

## ENABLERS

The enablers, also referred to as support, are the "reusable" resources of an organization and provide execution capabilities for the business processes. These are the three elements in the lower part of the Process Configuration Model:

- **Human Capital**. Competence is a standard requirement for an individual to properly perform a specific job. It encompasses a combination of knowledge, skills, and behavior utilized to getting work done. At the enterprise-level of an organization, the collective competence and capabilities of its employees is referred to as its Human Capital. In the context of the business processes, human capital means the deployment of capable people to optimally execute processes. Based on the required business process capabilities, competencies are defined for the process performers—who are then deployed to do the work and are measured and rewarded based on their performance. The professional practices here include: Organization Development and Design, Human Change Management, and Learning & Development.
- **Enabling Technology**. In the context of the process configuration, enabling technologies include information technology - systems and business applications, data stores, mechanisms such as production lines, robots, scientific equipment, and engineering equipment. Professional practices here include: Information Technology (Systems Development Life Cycle Methodology), and relevant Engineering and Science practices for processes-in-scope.

- **Supporting Infrastructure**. Infrastructure in the process configuration can be defined as the capital asset which enables all aspects of the business process configuration. This may range from facilities, communications, and technical platforms, to utilities and energy. The supporting professional practices vary by the type of infrastructure.

Thus, the Business Process Configuration model is a tool which facilitates the understanding, alignment, and improvement of all the elements dedicated to delivering organizational performance through streamlined processes and its guides and enablers.

## How to Use the Process Configuration Model

While this is not a substitute for a formal organization-wide methodology, it is a "poor person's process management methodology" for planning, analyzing, improving, and implementing process changes. This provides an easy to understand visual of how work gets done in an organization or in any of its parts. The model's practical use in the following outline is for all organizational roles involved in the management and support of business process assets.

- **Process Owners, Managers, and Workers**. To understand and analyze process components and monitor performance; identify gaps and opportunities for improvement; and promote common language through awareness of parts that make up the whole.
- **Project Managers**. To understand interdependencies and impact of change to create an initial project plan that would include performance objectives, areas for work breakdown structure (WBS), estimate of time and effort, and scope of stakeholders involved.
- **Process Practitioners**. This would include Business, Performance, and Technology Analysts. To identify scope and potential impact of change; plan for research and information gathering—including formulation of asking questions to interview relevant stakeholders; aligning and coordinating efforts of multiple professional practices involved in change.

## Key Points

- The Process Configuration Model describes all of the components that make up the workings of a process to deliver performance. Desired performance is delivered through the optimal use of the guiding and enabling components of the processes.

- This model provides an effective way of understanding process configuration, analyzing the components, and determining areas for improvement, along with identifying methods and tools needed to support each of the parts of the configuration.

- The model is also effective in process improvement projects: for initiating process improvement projects, creating a plan of action, estimating the cost, executing the components holistically through alignment of various professional practices, and delivering desired results.

Business drivers impact change to business processes, which in turn influence changes to the organization, technology, and supporting infrastructure. For successful implementation, all four of these factors must be holistically viewed, analyzed, and changed. A process-driven comprehensive methodology is needed to manage business change in any organization. See Figure 8.1, which will be referenced throughout this chapter.

**Figure 8.1 BPTrends Associates' BPM Methodology**

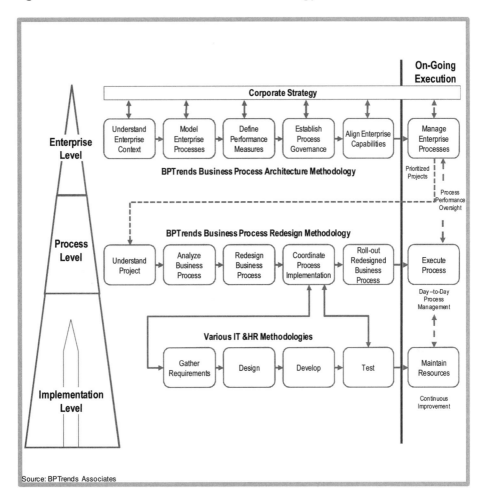

## *Methodology Overview*

There are many methodologies that analyze processes in their current state and propose a future state of transformation. These are primarily at the process-level of change, while providing some or little enterprise level context. A methodology that considers all parts of process change throughout the enterprise is essential. BPTrends Associates' BPM Methodology is such a comprehensive framework. It is composed of three integrated tiers of business process management and change - at the Enterprise Level, Process Level, and Implementation Level. Business changes begin with the organizational strategy, where senior executives analyze the state of the business, understand the business drivers, evaluate performance, and develop a business performance plan. See Figure 8.2.

**Figure 8.2 Business Change Impact**

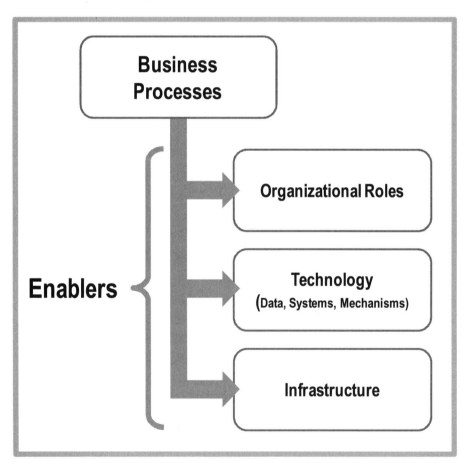

This plan must take a systemic view of organizational change, which is driven to achieve performance through execution of processes that are enabled by people and technology. We will examine the Framework to understand how the business process and its enablers "journey" through the "land" of business change.

Ideally, at the enterprise-level, the process understanding of BPM should facilitate change in product and service offerings, strategic intent, and core organizational capabilities. However, organizations where the senior executives do not value processes as an asset and understand that they drive change to other assets are not process-centric, and therefore are not likely to undertake enterprise level process change using any BPM approach. However, if some parts of the organization need to assess and change processes, they may still utilize the framework to reap the benefit of a methodical approach to process change. The framework can be utilized for various levels of organizational units; for example, corporate level, business unit level, or a division level. The selected level may be referred to as the Organization-in-Focus (OIF), and the processes to be worked on may be referred to as the Processes-in-Focus (PIF).

This chapter is not a tutorial, but rather an introduction to the methodology. However, in Chapter 12, one example is taken through the process-level steps of the methodology to demonstrate sample techniques and outputs. Detailed examples at the enterprise-level and at the implementation-level are out of scope for this book. Enterprise-level process assets are created by senior management, and implementation-level is where the enablers are implemented at a very detailed level. Process-level is the domain of all - senior managers to line managers, workers, and process professionals. This is the target audience for this book. Therefore, in Chapter 12, the process-level methodology is covered in detail to provide useful tools and techniques for your immediate use.

Let's examine the components of the framework.

## *Enterprise Level*

Facilitated by process professionals, use of the enterprise-level of the methodology is the responsibility of the senior management of an enterprise to create the process architecture and its supporting framework. The corporate strategy drives this part of the methodology. A brief description of the phases of the methodology is provided, along with the major steps to be undertaken.

### UNDERSTAND ENTERPRISE CONTEXT

A review of corporate strategy for the Organization-in-Focus is conducted in this phase. This phase includes understanding the OIF elements such as lines of business, business drivers, value proposition, its stakeholders and their expectations, and the future direction of the organization. Understanding these elements establishes a base line of where the organization is, where it is heading, and an overall context of 'how work gets done' – the macro-level processes and their known value chains. This phase should be conducted under the sponsorship of and in partnership with senior management representing cross-functional business and/or functional interest. The major steps within this phase include an understanding of:

- Business drivers and environment
- Enterprise-level stakeholders and their expectations
- Current state and future vision
- Performance gaps and strategies
- Capability needs: process, people, technology, systems, information, and infrastructure
- Known gaps and opportunities
- Various programs and projects underway.

### MODEL ENTERPRISE PROCESSES

Enterprise business processes are identified for the OIF starting with the stakeholders' perspective. If the OIF is the enterprise, then business value chains are identified (if they are not already known through the corporate strategic planning initiative). The enterprise-level stakeholders are identified so that we can understand the "outside looking in" view of the business, such as the customers and suppliers, followed by the internal stakeholders, such as employees and management.

The enterprise process model (that is, process architecture or a blueprint) would start by examining the current state of the business, followed by the creation of a future state view. The modeling pattern used for this level is: Core – Management – Support, as discussed in Chapter 6. End-to-end Level 1 processes are identified from the supplier stakeholders to the customer stakeholders. The Core is typically the "bread and butter" of the OIF; describing how the value proposition is delivered and the goals, such as revenue and market share, are achieved. Overlaying these core processes are one or more value chains, which can be the lines of business and/or routes to market. At this level, only summary-level flows among the processes are identified.

The next step includes the identification of Management and Support processes. Sometimes the value chains are identified at this stage—if they were not clearly defined or understood to start with. Each of the Level 1 processes is then broken down to their respective Level 2 processes. Typically, Levels 1 and 2 business process models, along with their definitions, constitute an organizational Business Process Architecture (Blueprint). See one example of a Blueprint in Chapter 3, Figure 3.2.

At the time that the enterprise processes are being analyzed and documented, a parallel exercise to develop an enterprise conceptual data model for the OIF, along with appropriate subject areas, should be undertaken. The fundamental data entities should be identified to facilitate identification of the data and information needs of the business processes. This output may be referred to as an *organizational data map* (the technical name would be conceptual data model). Remember, process and data go hand in hand; one without the other has little value.

Currently, the concept of conceptual data models is not considered to be a part of the process domain. As the discipline of process management is still evolving, it is my hope that the industry will understand the value of aligning the enterprise processes and enterprise conceptual data models into a single domain of knowledge—irrespective of how these disciplines are managed by current organizational structures. The detailed models that follow a conceptual data model (logical and physical data models) discussed in Chapter 6 would, of course, remain outside the scope of this domain.

The major steps within this phase include:

- Understanding value chains and lines of business
- Conducting stakeholders analysis to understand business interactions
- Identifying Level 1 core processes, summary flows between them, and management and support processes (and their definitions)
- Developing Level 2 business processes for each of the Level 1 processes—particularly the core processes (and their definitions)
- Identifying major data entities, subject areas, developing a conceptual data model, and mapping data subject areas and data entities to the business processes.

## DEFINE PERFORMANCE MEASURES

Driven by the organizational goals, performance measures are identified for each of the Level 1 processes and relevant value chains. The measures identified for the OIF must be aligned with the measures of the overall organization, as appropriate. Among the processes, measures should not conflict with each other. For example, Sales would like the product inventory to increase so that the product is always available for shipping to their customers, whereas Finance would not like to carry the cost of extra inventory on the books. One of the challenges will be how to deal with functional "vertical" measures versus process "horizontal" measures. The performance of executives is managed and rewarded by their functional area measures. Responsibility for process measures means changing the measurement and reward philosophy of the process owners, bringing new complexity by departing from the traditional approach, level of comfort, and compensation. This would require a change in the management model and governance practices.

The major steps within this phase include:

- Understanding the measures and goals of the OIF, how they align with the overall organization, and understanding related functional area measures
- Establishing measures for the Value Chains, Level 1 and Level 2 processes
- Aligning process measures to the organizational scorecard
- Developing a communication plan for the new measurement approach.

## ESTABLISH PROCESS GOVERNANCE

Establishing process governance begins with establishing business process ownership, a charter, and agreed upon measurements of the performance of the processes—all addressed in previous phases. This phase can become very politically charged, as the traditional measurement of executives will fundamentally change and will thus impact their domain of responsibility and reward system. To overcome resistance, very strong leadership and commitment is needed, along with an active partnership with Human Resources management.

While some organizations may become process-centric by breaking the functional silos, the vast majority settle on a hybrid approach. This approach may continue to have executives leading functional areas, as well as assigning ownership of one or more business processes to them. Some organizations create a council of process owners made up of the functional heads. The council governs the business process assets collaboratively.

The major steps within this phase include:

- Creating a process ownership charter and measurement approach
- Establishing a process owners council or forum and its method of operation
- Implementing a measurement and reward system for process owners

- Planning and allocating resources for managing process assets
- Providing direction for process performance improvement.

## ASSIGN PROCESS OWNERSHIP

The primary purpose of establishing process ownership is to ensure the boundaries of accountability are clearly defined at Levels 1 and 2 and the Value Chains. The executive process owners must plan for the measurement of process performance, monitor and measure performance, budget for improvements, obtain resources, and initiate projects for continuous improvement. They are also responsible for aligning the processes and ensuring cross-functional integration is streamlined (not being inhibited by the functional silos). Process owners must be accountable for business process performance, as well as the quality and integrity of data and information used and transformed by the process under his/her charge. Thus, the need for having a separate data owner or steward, as is the current practice, would become redundant. The rationale for this was covered in Chapter 6.

The major steps within this sub-phase include:

- Developing and agreeing on process and data ownership roles
- Establishing process owners for the value chains and Level 1 processes
- Identifying process owners/managers for Level 2 processes
- Developing a process owner charter that includes management across functional areas
- Communicating the process owner charter and how ways of working would impact process accountabilities.

## ALIGN ENTERPRISE CAPABILITIES

All work is accomplished through business processes supported by their guides and enablers. This includes products and services, brands, capital, people, information, technology, application systems, and infrastructure. All of the business model components discussed in Chapter 1 must be understood, defined, and aligned to the enterprise processes and delivery mechanisms through programs and projects.

The major steps within this phase include:

- Understanding enterprise business model components and needs for their alignment
- Understanding the process capabilities and their alignment needs
- Aligning organizational strategies with human capital, information and knowledge, enabling technologies, and the supporting infrastructure
- Aligning all programs and projects impacting process change.

## MANAGE ENTERPRISE PROCESSES

Managing enterprise processes gives rise to the need for establishing a center of excellence or a business process office similar to Finance for managing cash assets and Human Resources for managing human capital. Among others, the role of this organization entity would be to facilitate monitoring and managing business process performance. This organizational entity would assist in monitoring process performance, identifying issues and opportunities for improvement, and shaping projects for process change. In addition, this group would maintain the business process blueprint on behalf of the process owners and ensure accessibility by all employees. The group would provide to project managers and their teams process orientation, training, and support in applying the methodology and standards, and use of the supporting tools. This group needs to have close collaboration and alignment with the activities of the Project Management Office (PMO), which manages enterprise-wide project schedules and facilitates allocation of resources. The prioritization of processes is done at the enterprise Levels 1 and 2. However, even if lower-level processes such as Level 3 are to be improved, this group would provide guidance in the context of the superior processes.

Business processes are identified for improvement based on the need to maintain effectiveness and efficiency of organizational capabilities and also to meet the needs of the future state vision, goals, and supporting strategies. The processes are prioritized because there is "pain". That is, the processes and their enablers are not performing up to the expected measures, or "gain", so there is a significant benefit to improving the process and its enablers.

The major steps within this phase include:

- Establishing a business process services office charter (center of excellence)
- Establishing and supporting methodology, standards, tools, and a repository of process knowledge
- Providing training and coaching to project managers and teams
- Monitoring process performance and reporting to process owners
- Facilitating overall assessment and improvement of the process blueprint.

## Process Level

To improve the performance of the processes or to redesign for innovation, programs or projects for change are created by senior management, or line managers. These programs/projects can be initiated due to some business change or a gap in performance. Facilitated by process professionals, or by the managers themselves, this part of the methodology would be utilized. A brief description is provided, along with major steps to be undertaken in each phase of the methodology.

### ASSIGN PROJECT MANAGEMENT

When a specific process has been identified for improvement, a project manager is identified to lead the effort, along with an initial set of team members. The project manager would typically be one of the process managers assigned to this role by the process owner. The project manager and the team are responsible for utilizing suitable professional practices to execute the business process change and its supporting enablers: organizational roles (people), technology (applications and other mechanisms), and infrastructure (support for all capabilities). Here, the project management professional practice is the overall umbrella under which the other required professional practices are deployed. While the practice of project management and its methodologies are universal in nature, there are some unique attributes of process change which must be led by the manager and understood by the team members and all relevant key stakeholders. Some of the unique attributes to be considered are:

- In addition to the need of project stakeholders to successfully execute the project, the focus of this initiative involves business process stakeholders—those who are impacted by the process and would be affected by the change. While in some cases, employees would benefit from change in that they would gain opportunities to develop themselves, in other cases, the consequences of the change, such as broader job responsibilities or loss of jobs is a business reality to be managed, and managed well.

- The project teams may be cross-functional, cross-business units, and cross geographies, with the members drawn from the functional areas touched by the process.

- Process improvement projects are unlike other project initiatives, where the project objectives and scope are relatively clear in the beginning. In process improvement, while the initial project objectives may be outlined, the scope of the change effort is ambiguous until some level of analysis is conducted to understand the impact of the process and its enablers.

- Project managers, project management such as champions and sponsors, team members, and process stakeholders must be familiar with the business process change practice and its implications along the execution of the various allied methodologies such as Organization Design, Human Change Management, and application of Lean practice.

- A process improvement methodology must be agreed upon, along with an understanding of other related professional practices and their roles along the process improvement journey.

- Build a team environment for overall understanding, cooperation, and engagement by all team members, relevant business stakeholders, and professional practices analysts. This membership is likely to be cross-functional, cross-business units, and cross-geographies.

## UNDERSTAND PROJECT

Begin with the end in mind. The purpose of this phase is to understand the scope of the change in the process and its enablers and to define the vision of the future state: what the process capability would be like when it performs at its best. Irrespective of the level of the process in a hierarchy, the first thing is to understand the process context: its "ancestry" or superior process, and its "siblings", the processes that may be interdependent. This is where a Business Process Blueprint is extremely useful in understanding the context. Process stakeholders are identified and their expectations harnessed for process performance in the form of a vision for the future state. Process scope is then developed by identifying all the inputs, outputs, guides and enablers, and process touch points, both upstream and downstream. A high-level process health assessment is then conducted to provide insights for scoping the project with relevant details.

The major steps within this phase include:

- Understanding process context and stakeholders
- Developing stakeholders' expectation of process performance – a vision
- Developing process scope, along with all enablers and touch points
- Conducting a high-level process health check for identifying issues and opportunities
- Developing project scope to marshal resources and gain agreement for the next step.

## ANALYZE BUSINESS PROCESS

Perform *Process Archeology*, which means digging for facts. The purpose of this phase is to understand how work is done in the scoped process, along with facts about how it performs currently and any gaps, based on the stakeholders' expectations and vision. Business process models are developed for the process and its enablers only to the extent of the issues understood by the team. Exhaustive analysis is not recommended in this phase (I use a Japanese term "Toriaezu" to limit over analysis...the term roughly means "It's OK for now!") Using various techniques, such as Root

Cause Analysis, Redesign, and Lean Six Sigma, issues and opportunities are identified ("pain and gain"). Some improvements, known as quick wins, which provide immediate benefits without much effort, are identified and planned for implementation.

The major steps within this phase include:

- Developing process models in the as-is state and identifying major data entities
- Measuring current performance and comparing against the vision
- Conducting root cause analysis and understanding pains and possible gains
- Identifying and implementing quick wins
- Presenting/gaining management agreement and preparing for redesign phase.

## REDESIGN BUSINESS PROCESS

Innovate and create a feasible design. This is the phase where new ways of working are explored to gain competitive advantage for process performance enhancement and its sustainability. First, industry trends are understood and benchmarks are analyzed to determine possibilities for future processes and their enablers, such as organizational design and technology. Business process redesign criteria are then identified from the vision, gaps in performance, and other learnings. They will be used as a guide when developing improved processes. Brainstorming for possible solutions is conducted and a process model for the redesign possibilities is created. These multiple possible solutions are called could-be processes.

At this time, all relevant constraints, such as the feasibility of design, resources, and time, are considered to determine which of the recommended solutions will become the to-be design. The to-be design is validated for its practicality to gain confidence in the solution. The to-be process design is finalized and should be accompanied by a conceptual data model showing data needs at a high-level. A business case for the recommended change in process and its enablers is developed, including cost benefit analysis, risk analysis, and a high-level transformation plan. Management makes go/no-go decisions based on the business case.

The major steps within this phase include:

- Benchmarking and understanding trends in process and its enablers
- Understanding capabilities: process, organization, technology, and infrastructure
- Conducting ideation for process innovation
- Developing could-be models and a to-be process design (validate feasibility)
- Developing business case for change for the process and its enablers (includes high-level transformation plan)
- Presenting/gaining management agreement and preparing for implementation.

## COORDINATE PROCESS IMPLEMENTATION

Design the specifications for construction. This phase drives the development of specifications for changes to processes, which are then passed on for creating solutions for the guides and enablers, including organizational roles, data, and applications. The business users, assisted by the appropriate analysts, identify data requirements, business rules, and functional requirements for the applications—the automation of the process using information technology. Competencies are identified for effective performance of the process. These competencies become the basis for developing organizational design—the roles of people to be aligned to the process and the development of role profiles, job descriptions, and process training.

The major steps within this phase include:

- Planning implementation phase
- Developing process specifications for implementation
- Delegating development tasks to other groups
- Creating management and measurement systems for redesigned process

- Assembling, integrating, and testing all elements of redesigned process.

## *Implementation Level*

The specifications for the process and its enablers are designed, developed, tested, and implemented in this phase. Each of the professional practices has its own methodology that is deployed at this level. For example, Systems Development Life Cycle Methodology for IT, Organization Design for people roles and responsibilities, and Human Change Management for changing behaviors to accept the change.

The business processes are documented in detail, training is developed and delivered to all process performers, process changes are implemented where applicable, and communications to all process stakeholders is executed. Upon roll out, the process is reviewed. An after action review for small changes, and a post implementation review for large changes are conducted to capture learnings for future use.

All process knowledge is preserved so that it may be reused by employees, process performers, managers, owners, and other projects. Any additional recommendations for process improvements are documented and handed over to the process owners for inclusion in the next cycle of change. This phase works in conjunction with the Implementation-Level for the alignment of change to all the enablers.

## Key Points

- Business change impacts business processes, which in turn impact their enablers: people, technology, and infrastructure. All these factors must be holistically analyzed and changed for success.

- For an organization to become process-centric through the realization that business processes are a critical asset, a comprehensive BPM methodology must be identified and implemented. This methodology framework must address the three tiers of business process management: Enterprise-level, Process-Level, and Implementation-Level.

- An Enterprise-Level methodology can be utilized for an overall organization, a business unit or a division. The scope is called Organization-In-Focus (OIF). The selected processes may be referred to as Processes-In-Focus (PIF).

Business process improvement is a collaborative effort among several professional practices, supported by specialists who contribute a variety of skills. The professional practices include Strategic Planning, Program and Project Management, Business Process Management (BPM), Organization Development & Design (OD), and Technologies, including Information Technology (IT). The roles of the practitioners in terms of processes support may include: *Process Owner* for Strategic Planning, business workers and managers for process improvement responsibility, *Process Analyst* for process redesign, *Business Analyst* for functional analysis, and *Technology Analyst* for systems. The role titles of individuals in these roles vary across organizations.

This chapter describes the core effectiveness and functional competencies required for the above-mentioned roles that support business process and allied disciplines. For common understanding, the roles are grouped under generic categories. Other behavioral competencies and softer skills are out of scope in this chapter.

## *Competency Explanation*

Competency may be defined as a demonstration of proficient behavior in the execution of tasks or activities that require unique knowledge, skills, and motivation in their usage.

### Knowledge + Skills + (Motivation/Attitude/Opportunity) = Behavior

For any activity, a person must have knowledge of the subject and develop the how-to skills to do something with that knowledge; then they must be motivated to use their knowledge and skills by application. When this behavior is consistently demonstrated by an individual, it may be stated that the person is now competent in that subject. Having only the knowledge or just the skills does not make someone competent. Having knowledge and skills but not the motivation to apply them means a person cannot develop a behavior of proficiency.

Studies at Center for Creative Leadership have shown that a learning framework known as "70/20/10" describes the formula for building competencies: 10% of learning takes place through formal training, 20% occurs by working with other experts in the field, and 70% takes place by doing, that is, by applying the knowledge and skills. The main take-away is that just by going to formal training in a subject does not make someone competent. There must be practical application of those learnings, as well.

There are two types of competencies: *Effectiveness* and *Functional*. The effectiveness competencies include business and decision making capabilities, along with softer skills such as communication and interpersonal skills. The functional competencies include subject matter-based expertise, including the technical skills needed to accomplish a desired activity. Business workers, managers, and executives need both the effectiveness and functional competencies at a level of proficiency that is appropriate for their role in the organization.

## BPM Competency Framework ("Mahal Framework")

The BPM Competency Framework is designed to address both the effectiveness and functional competencies needed by all the roles related to business process management and its allied professional practices. The roles in the framework are structured into generic groups within the two classifications. Each describes the purpose of its role: Process Owners, Process Managers, and Process Performers *drive process change;* Process Practitioners, Organization Designers, and Technology Practitioners *facilitate change.*

Table 9.1 describes what each role does. It is followed by Table 9.2, which contains the matrix of specific competencies for each role and the level of competency expected of a person in the role. The competencies are classified under Effectiveness and Functional types. This matrix is a guide for the organizations and individuals who want to plan their professional development in BPM. A detailed definition of each of the competencies is not in the scope of this book.

**Table 9.1 BPM Framework Roles**

| Role | Includes |
|---|---|
| **Process Owner**<br>*(Drives process change)* | Process Executives accountable for the strategy, performance, budgeting, and improvement of business processes |
| **Process Manager**<br>*(Drives process change)* | Managers responsible for the day-to-day execution of the process, reporting status, and recommending improvements |
| **Process Performer**<br>*(Drives process change)* | Business Workers assigned to support and execute the processes |
| **Process Practitioner**<br>*(Facilitate change)* | Process Analysts, Business Analysts, Business Data Analysts, Lean, Six Sigma, and Quality Control Specialists, Performance Analysts |
| **Organization Designer**<br>*(Facilitate change)* | Human Performance and Organization Development & Design Specialists |
| **Technology Practitioner**<br>*(Facilitate change)* | Technology Analysts and Process Engineers involved in the development and implementation of technology solutions |

The matrix in Table 9.2 is a recommended set for the individuals and organizations to plan and build their BPM knowledge, skills, and competencies. As organizations are at various levels of maturity in becoming process-centric, this matrix is not a "one size fits all" solution; rather, it is a checklist that should prompt informed discussion and, hopefully, promote action to include some of these in the respective development plans of the individuals and a criteria for building a center of excellence capability.

In the competency framework in Table 9.2, the first column represents competencies needed by the employees applying various Profession Practices. These practices are grouped under two types: Effectiveness and Functional. The effectiveness competencies enable individuals to perform irrespective of the nature of the industry. Typically, these are non-technical, but can be specific to a professional practice; for example Communication. Functional competencies always pertain to a professional practice and include specialized and/or technical skills and experience, such as technology development. The legend pertains to each of the columns that represent a role. These roles, as described in Table 9.1, are grouped to differentiate which roles drive change versus those that facilitate change.

Table Legend:

K – Must have knowledge

S – Must have skills (This includes knowledge)

C – Must have competency (includes knowledge, skills and experiential proficiency)

**Table 9.2 BPM Competency Framework "Mahal Framework"**

| Effectiveness Competencies | Competency | Drive Process Change | | | Facilitate Change | | |
|---|---|---|---|---|---|---|---|
| | | Process Owner | Process Manager | Process Performer | Process Practitioner | Organization Designer | Technology Practitioner |
| Strategic Planning | Business Acumen | C | C | C | C | C | C |
| | BPM Principles & Practice | C | C | C | C | C | C |
| | Stakeholders Focus | C | C | C | C | C | C |
| Strategic Execution | Managing Vision & Purpose | C | C | K | S | S | S |
| | Planning & Organizing | C | C | S | C | C | C |
| | Business Change Management | C | C | K | C | C | K |
| | Communication | C | C | C | C | C | C |

| Effectiveness Competencies | Competency | Drive Process Change | | | Facilitate Change | | |
|---|---|---|---|---|---|---|---|
| | | Process Owner | Process Manager | Process Performer | Process Practitioner | Organization Designer | Technology Practitioner |
| | Risk Management | C | C | C | C | C | C |
| Facilitation | Information Gathering, Research, & Facilitation | K | S | K | C | C | C |

| Functional Competencies | Competency | Drive Process Change | | | Facilitate Change | | |
|---|---|---|---|---|---|---|---|
| | | Process Owner | Process Manager | Process Performer | Process Practitioner | Organization Designer | Technology Practitioner |
| Business Process Management (BPM) | Business Process Management | C | C | K | C | C | K |

| Functional Competencies | Drive Process Change | | | Facilitate Change | | |
|---|---|---|---|---|---|---|
| Competency | Process Owner | Process Manager | Process Performer | Process Practitioner | Organization Designer | Technology Practitioner |
| Business Process Architecture | K | S | K | C | K | K |
| Process Modeling, Analysis & Innovation | K | S | K | C | K | K |
| Process Conceptual Data Modeling | K | S | K | C | K | S |
| Process Improvement Facilitation | K | K | K | C | K | K |
| Methods & Tools – Lean Six Sigma | K | S | K | C | K | S |
| Project Management for BPM | C | C | K | C | S | S |

| Functional Competencies | Competency | Drive Process Change | | | Facilitate Change | | |
|---|---|---|---|---|---|---|---|
| | | Process Owner | Process Manager | Process Performer | Process Practitioner | Organization Designer | Technology Practitioner |
| | Data Modeling & Business Rules | K | S | K | C | K | S |
| Organization Development (OD) | Organizational Design & Effectiveness | S | S | K | K | C | K |
| | Business Transition Management | C | S | K | S | C | S |
| | Training | S | S | S | C | C | C |
| Technology Development | Project Management for Technical Development | K | K | K | K | K | C |
| | Requirements Gathering & Analysis | K | K | K | S | K | C |

| Functional Competencies | Competency | Drive Process Change | | | Facilitate Change | | |
|---|---|---|---|---|---|---|---|
| | | Process Owner | Process Manager | Process Performer | Process Practitioner | Organization Designer | Technology Practitioner |
| | Technology Solutions | K | K | K | K | K | C |
| Business Process Management Systems (BPMS) | Application Design & Development | K | C | S | C | K | S |
| | Application Implementation | K | K | K | C | K | C |

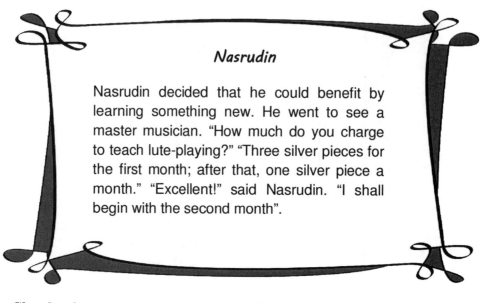

## Nasrudin

Nasrudin decided that he could benefit by learning something new. He went to see a master musician. "How much do you charge to teach lute-playing?" "Three silver pieces for the first month; after that, one silver piece a month." "Excellent!" said Nasrudin. "I shall begin with the second month".

Clearly there are no short cuts such as Nasrudin suggested! The development of competency is accomplished through planning, learning, and application. I always emphasize that "Self-development is Self-accountability!"

## Key Points

- Several professional practices are involved in the Business Process Management discipline. In these practices, the variety of special roles is still evolving in terms of their alignment among other allied roles for collective and collaborative service to the organizations. It is critical that some mutual core competencies be defined for these roles so that their efforts are collaborative and effective.

- Competency may be defined as a demonstration of proficient behavior in the execution of tasks or activities that require unique skills. Knowledge + Skills + (Motivation/Attitude/Opportunity) = Behavior/Competency.

- To effectively develop competencies, workers must plan their development and build those skills. As a general rule, a person can develop roughly two competencies in a calendar year. "Self-development is Self-accountability!"

Assets in an organization are managed by appropriately funded organization units who have the charter to deploy professional practices and optimize the value of those assets in fulfilling the mission and delivering the value proposition to its customers. A Finance Group, headed by a Chief Financial Officer and supported by financial practices and tools, manages the capital assets of an organization; The Human Resources Group, headed by, say, a Vice President of HR, deploys best practices for managing human capital; and a Facilities Group, headed by the director of facilities, uses facilities management practices to manage the facilities of the organization. Therefore, it follows that there should be a Business Process Services Group, headed by a Business Process Officer, to deploy best practices and tools in support of Business Process Management.

## *Business Process Services Organization*

To support the professional practice of Business Process Management (BPM), an organization should have a go-to organizational entity where workers, managers, management, analysts, and project teams can seek advice, training, coaching, and other assistance in the application of methods and tools for improving processes. Many organizations establish a go-to organization unit for Information Technology (IT) as their BPM discipline evolves. IT plays a custodial role because the process discipline helps their mission of developing applications. As an understanding of process assets becomes pervasive among business management and they realize that they, not IT, own the process assets, a business support organizational entity is created within the business, itself. Sometimes it is practical to move some of the IT analysts to the business organization unit for cross-pollination of knowledge and expertise in process orientation.

The support organization unit may be given various labels. I prefer to name and brand such an entity with a clear perception that they are a "service" organization, not a "bureaucracy" that "tells" projects what to do. While many names are used, such as Center of Excellence, Business Process Center, Business Process Office, I prefer to call this entity: Business Process Services.

This support entity must be treated like any other organization unit. To be successful, it must have a business model, including mission, vision, strategies, measures, a clear definition of its customers, products and services, and operational ways of working. While there are many ways to develop such an organization structure, following is a practical approach for creating the charter of Business Process Services. My objective is not to provide a solution, but rather to provide ideas to think about for the formation of a business process support service. The organization unit that manages process assets must be appropriately positioned in the business and appropriately funded and staffed.

### Nasrudin

Nasrudin bought a donkey. Someone told him that he would have to give it a certain amount of feed every day. This he considered to be too much. He would experiment, he decided, to get it used to less food. Each day therefore, he reduced its rations. Eventually, when the donkey was reduced to almost no food at all, it fell over and died. "Pity." said Nasrudin. "If I had a little more time before it died, I could have gotten it accustomed to living on nothing at all."

Similarly, "starving" Business Process Services of either management support or funding reduces the value of this organization entity and its effectiveness in supporting process assets.

## VALUE PROPOSITION

Three dimensions are critical for creating the value proposition for an organizational unit's stakeholders, including the overall organization itself: Customer Intimacy, Products & Service Leadership, and Operational Excellence. See Figure 10.1. The concept of three dimensions is based on Michael Treacy and Fred Wiersema's study, and has been widely used in the business management discipline.

**Figure 10.1 Value Proposition Model**

## CUSTOMER INTIMACY

Customer intimacy is about identifying customers and their needs, then building a trusting relationship for long-term growth and loyal partnership through the delivery of valued products and services. The first step is to identify the customers, both internal and external, for the value proposition. Group the customers according to the type of their requirements. For example, BPM "education and training" could be one group that serves various stakeholders such as senior executives, managers, and other professionals. Next, for each of the customer groupings, identify the unique value proposition and areas of support that need to be provided by the Business Process Services (BPS) Group. This clarifies what products and services the customers expect in support of their roles in the organization.

## PRODUCTS & SERVICES INNOVATION AND LEADERSHIP

The term leadership implies innovation in developing and offering unique solutions to customers that satisfy promised value in product and service offerings. This second step is to identify what BPS has to offer in terms of products and services. What products and services will provide effectiveness in delivering the value proposition to the customers? For each of those offerings, identify categories of support and a menu of offerings. Ask this question: what products and services will be put in place to directly contribute to the success of Customer Intimacy. This will provide a clear set of products and services for delivering the value proposition.

## OPERATIONAL EXCELLENCE

This step constitutes how BPS operates and makes optimal use of its capabilities, including processes, people, and technology. Processes include the effective engagement of BPS analysts with their customers and delivery of promised services; People include the organizational roles, their competencies, and optimal ways of working for success. And technology includes methods and tools in support of the overall capability.

In my experience, once these three dimensions are identified and understood, the BPS Mission falls out easily. If the Mission is defined first, it may actually inhibit innovative thinking around the three dimensions. The next logical step is to create the BPS Vision. It is based on the value proposition and customer expectations, followed by Key Performance Indicators (KPIs) that measure achievement of the vision. To achieve the Vision, strategies with clear objectives are crafted, followed by identification of programs and projects to execute the strategies. This follows the approach addressed in Chapter 1.

As in any other organization, a management structure that includes a reporting hierarchy, budgeting, and measurements needs to be put in place. BPS could be made part of an existing organization unit, reporting to an existing management structure—preferably at the senior executive level. The BPS group should work in coordination with a Program Management Office (PMO). To institutionalize BPS in a large organization can take anywhere from three to five years. Proper branding and marketing is needed to "sell" BPM and BPS to all the customer groups and management. Selling the value proposition is an on-going process requiring a "missionary" approach in that one must continue to spread awareness and education, irrespective of the hurdles encountered due to "non believers" in methodical process management.

In bygone days, there was a salesman who would go around neighborhoods selling household goods door-to-door to the housewives. One housewife was particularly annoyed at the salesman for knocking on her door and interrupting her household chores. She told the salesman that she did not want anything and slammed the door on him. The salesman fell back and his hat fell off onto the lawn. The salesman got up, put his hat on his head, and with the bag of his goodies knocked on the door of the same lady. The lady, more annoyed, shouted, "Go away!!!" She pushed him back again and slammed the door. This went on three times. After the third time, the salesman again put his hat on his head, adjusted his tie, and, wearing a forced smile, knocked on the door. When the lady opened the door, the salesman said, "Madam, let's stop kidding around. Let me show you some interesting items I have to sell".

Process practitioners need the patience and thick skin that salesman had. Perseverance and a belief that process is an asset of the organization will enable them to continually sell and not give up when "thrown out" by project managers and teams who don't understand the importance of a process discipline—the "invisible asset".

## *Business Process Services Example*

The examples in Table 10.1 and Table 10.2 of a BPS Value Proposition are outlined to provide a map of the potential artifacts. This is not intended to be the only solution. It is a model of how the value proposition could be created for your own organization. It should be adjusted and adapted for your own organization and circumstances.

**Table 10.1 Customer Intimacy**

| Customer Group | Value Proposition | Support Features |
|---|---|---|
| Senior Management and Process Owners | Strategic business process alignment and performance | Develop process architecture; Assist in governance, measurements, and alignment of capabilities; help prioritize process changes |
| Business Process Managers | Effective business performance delivery | Facilitate identification of process change initiatives, provide process mapping and measurement support |
| Process Performers | Enhance ways of working and promote reusability of knowledge | Provide education and training in improvement methods and tools; provide access to process definitions |
| Project Managers & Project Teams | Assist project success through methodical application of methods and tools | Provide education and training; guidance, coaching, methods, and tools; process knowledge for reusability of resources |

| Customer Group | Value Proposition | Support Features |
|---|---|---|
| Allied Professional Groups (process practitioners, organization designers, technology practitioners) | Collaborate in design, development, and implementation of solutions to process guides and enablers | Provide BPM methodology, tools expertise, and training in all three levels of process management: enterprise, process, and implementation |

**Table 10.2 Product & Services Leadership**

| Offerings | Value Proposition |
|---|---|
| Awareness and Training | Process orientation; training and education modules; train-the-trainer to create internal change agents |
| Consultation and Facilitation | Guide & coach as internal consultants; facilitate information gathering and group facilitations |
| Methods and Tools | Business Process Management methodology; process modeling and analysis tools; process knowledge repository |
| Decision Making Support | Performance monitoring, prioritization analysis, and decision making tools |

## OPERATIONAL EXCELLENCE

**Process**: Team Ways of Working

- Market products & services to internal groups (how the analysts would reach out to the managers and project teams across the organization to make them aware of their services)

- Customer engagement process (the protocols of participating in project teams and charging for services based on corporate philosophy)
- Measures and continuous improvement (identifying, measuring, and reporting key measures of success such as KPI's, and planning for continuous improvement in BPS' own processes)

**People**: Organization Roles & Responsibilities

- Organization design structure - design of BPS' own structure, including roles and responsibilities in alignment with internal client groups such as business units
- BPM & allied competencies definition and development - maintain the competency framework discussed in Chapter 9, advise other employees in their development plans, and develop BPS' own employees in relevant competencies
- Team effectiveness - develop, maintain, and nurture a high performing team of BPS' employees

**Methodology**: Methods and Tools

- Analysis, modeling and design tools - identify relevant and effective BPM methodology and tools, get trained in their use, and support the organizational needs
- Information gathering and facilitation methods and tools - become proficient in the practice of facilitation, including group and remote, and enable others to do the same
- Process knowledge repository - determine standards for process knowledge management and storage, and make the process models and their definitions available to the organization

Having defined the three dimensions, develop the Mission of the Business Process Services organization unit. From the customer value proposition and support offerings, develop a Vision—the projected future state of the group's mission. Identify Key Performance Indictors to track and measure the success of the group in providing the promised value proposition.

Once the business model is defined, the BPS should identify its strategies and programs to deliver the promised vision. One of the critical strategies should be of branding and marketing BPS to all relevant stakeholders in the organization. The next step would be to gain management approvals and build the BPS capabilities.

## Key Points

- To support the professional practice of Business Process Management (BPM), an organization should have a go-to organizational entity where workers, managers, management, analysts, and project teams can seek advice, training, coaching, and other assistance in the application of methods and tools for improving processes.

- Within the domain of the overall organization, the Business Process Services group must define and develop their business model, identify strategies and programs to deliver valuable services to management, project teams, and employees at all levels of the organization. The Business Model should include: value proposition, mission, vision, guiding principles, and organization structure. The strategies should include BPM awareness and training, methods and tools, products and services, and marketing of support to the projects.

- BPM concepts, its value to the business, and the support services it provides must be continuously marketed within the organization for sustainability. The BPM mantra needs to be "sell better, faster, cheaper, agile, competitive solutions around how work gets done." Everyday ...Sell, Sell, Sell!

- Chinese proverb: Talk does not cook rice. So, plan your work and work your plan.

There are two broad areas of process enabling tools and technology. Business processes are enabled by application systems software for individual or enterprise-wide applications such as ERP (Enterprise Resource Planning), and there are also software tools that enable the analysis, design, automation, and monitoring of business processes. The first area of business software is out of scope for this book, but a brief outline is provided on the type of current tool sets used by business process practitioners in this continually changing market place.

Most of this chapter is copied from BPTrends' report on the state of software tools, *The State of Business Process Management, 2010*; February 2010, Celia Wolf and Paul Harmon.

There is currently a significant challenge in defining software tools because the evolutionary nature of tools is such that they are evolving to support the various needs of the business process discipline. There are lots of small- and mid-sized vendors offering specialized modeling or rules tools; there are mid-sized vendors offering more or less sophisticated BPMS tools; and there are large vendors, like IBM, Oracle, SAP, and Microsoft, who are working to define an even more comprehensive BPM platform that will include not only tools, but also extensive new infrastructure capabilities. The major types of business process software tools are:

- Simple Graphics Tools
- Business Process Modeling Tools (BP Modeling Tools)
- Organization Modeling Tools
- Business Process Simulation Tools
- Business Process Management Suites or Systems (BPMS Tools)
- Business Process Management Applications (BPM Applications)
- Business Process Monitoring Tools
- Rule Management Tools

## *Simple Graphics Tools*

A significant portion of the companies seeking to describe or document business processes use either Word to create outlines, or graphics tools like Visio or PowerPoint. The advantage these tools offer is simplicity and familiarity. Most business managers already have them and are familiar with their use. The disadvantage of these products is that they are not designed to create a database or repository that can save and accumulate information about business processes. Thus, they tend to be used on isolated business process projects. It is nearly impossible to maintain business process documentation in these tools, so redesigns done using these products tend to be useless for subsequent redesign projects or for the development of enterprise process architecture. The following sections describe the types of software tools used by business process practitioners.

## *Business Process Modeling Tools*

Business process modeling tools are designed to not only define and document business processes, but to store information about the processes so that they can be easily updated and maintained. Companies that move beyond isolated process change efforts and decide to define enterprise-wide process architectures, almost always shift to one of these tools. They are more difficult to learn but the benefits they provide far outweigh the effort required.

## *Organization Modeling Tools*

Many BP modeling tools include features that allow users to create models of their organization. In essence, these models are very high-level views of how the organization interacts with its environment, what value chains and major business processes it supports, and how high-level processes are aligned with various types of enterprise resources. Many of the BP modeling tools include these capabilities, while some tools specialize in organization modeling.

## Business Process Simulation Tools

Most BP modeling tools include simulation capabilities—the technique of conducting "what if" analysis to test potential models and their solutions. In addition, there are some tools that are especially designed for more demanding simulation work. Most BP modeling teams turn to specialists to undertake simulation studies, and those specialists often prefer the more sophisticated simulation tools.

## Business Process Management Suites or Systems

These tools combine process modeling with runtime execution. In essence, they combine features previously found in workflow and EAI (Enterprise Application Integration) products. In some cases, the tools also incorporate rule management and process monitoring capabilities. These tools are newer and are just beginning to gain a foothold in companies engaged in BPM. In the long run, they promise to help companies create a process layer between those who define and manage processes and the software resources used to implement processes.

## Business Process Management Applications

In essence, BPM suites are tools that are used to create Business Process Management applications. A BPM application is an application that manages all of the people and software systems used to implement a specific process. Whenever the organization is called upon to execute a specific process, it relies on the BPM application to manage the execution. In a few years, as BPMS become more widely used, we expect to see applications offered with BPMS built-in. Business Process Management (BPM) is the discipline of understanding and optimizing processes as an asset of an organization for efficiency, effectiveness, competitive advantage, and sustainability. Business Process Management Systems (BPMS) are software enablers for the execution of processes. We expect ERP and CRM vendors to offer BPM applications especially designed to integrate with their current ERP or CRM modules. A BPMS is only a tool for building a BPM application. A BPM application is designed to execute a specific process with BPMS built to enable managers to modify the application as needed.

## Business Process Monitoring Tools

Most BPMS tools offer some process monitoring capabilities. They tend, for example, to provide information about process events to the process supervisors. Other BPMS tools, and more sophisticated monitoring tools, combine data from specific processes with information derived from other sources in a data warehouse and then use simulation techniques or Business Intelligence (BI) or data mining techniques to abstract patterns from the data and to report this "overview" information to executives via executive dashboards in something close to real-time. These tools are sometimes called Business Activity Monitoring (BAM) tools.

## Rule Management Tools

Most BP Modeling tools allow analysts to identify and save business rules. Most BPMS tools incorporate rule management tools that at least allow for the identification of business rules used in specific business processes. In some cases, the rule management tools can be used to actually analyze business rules at runtime and generate or suggest decisions using logical inferencing techniques.

## Innovators

Geoffrey Moore is a high tech marketing guru who has been involved in numerous technology launches. He wrote a very popular book, *Crossing the Chasm* (Harper Business, 1991), which describes the lifecycle of new technologies and the problems they face gaining widespread acceptance.

New technologies, according to Moore, are initially adopted by innovators: companies that are focused on new technologies and are willing to work hard to make a new technology work in order to gain an early advantage. Innovators have their own teams of sophisticated technologists and are willing to work with academics and vendors to create highly tailored solutions.

## Key Points

- BPMS (Business Process Management Systems) is not BPM (Business Process Management). Business Process Management is the discipline of understanding and optimizing processes as an asset of an organization for efficiency, effectiveness, competitive advantage, and sustainability. Business Process Management Systems are software enablers for the execution of processes.

- "Walk before you run", is a good approach for those who are early adopters of business process improvement enabling software. In a relatively inexpensive way, it is useful to understand the needs of an organization's process improvement initiatives and help develop ideas for standards and practices in analysis, modeling, redesign, and documentation of process knowledge. This also enables process practitioners to experiment and show, by example, the value of tools and their capabilities.

- Tools are only as good as the person using the tool in the most effective way. Understanding and usage of the tools should be a core competency for process practitioners to perform their job and also be able to provide orientation to all relevant users and resources.

Following is an example of the process-level methodology steps for the improvement of a process for the fictitious company NewAge Foods. The process used in the example is **Recruit and Hire Employees** process. The purpose of this chapter is to show examples of some of the key deliverables and the rationale behind each step in the methodology.

The details presented in this example are not a complete solution; in some cases there are sample templates to demonstrate what type of analysis and deliverables might be appropriate. Also, using the methodology, I have shown only one practical way of executing the steps; there may be other complementary steps based on the preferences of the professional change facilitators.

In this chapter, while the facilitation methods are referred to in the context of group facilitation, both interviewing and remote facilitation techniques are out of scope in this book. As the project management steps drive the process improvement methodology steps, the distinction is shown in the checklist. This is done to ensure clarity from the natural confusion between the steps of project management and process improvement.

## *Recruitment Issues*

In this fictitious example, sponsored by NewAge Foods' Vice President of Human Resources, a business/process analyst had conducted focus groups to identify issues around the acquisition of good talent in a timely manner. The following issues were identified by interviewing some key managers, employees, and human resource staff members:

- **Job Offer Delays**. The time between the final interview and a job offer is 8 weeks; candidates pursue other options and the company loses potentially good talent.

- **Quality of New Hires**. Some of the new hires, when assigned to expected roles, are not able to perform at the level expected of their positions.
- **Talent Acquisition**. The third party recruitment company is not providing timely and quality talent (the competition might be providing better commission and terms!).
- **Position Requisition**. The job descriptions submitted by the hiring managers are inconsistent and incomplete (the internal website is not very intuitive and does not provide a good help feature).
- **Managerial Approval**. Internal candidates do not get approval from their existing managers prior to applying for a job.
- **Interview Panel**. The interview panel is not thorough and not consistent in evaluating candidates based on organizational core competences.
- **Human Resources (HR) Roles**. The Human Resources staff serves several geographically dispersed business units; those who are near to the shared services office seem to get preferential attention. Candidates, both internal and external, do not know who to contact for inquiries about the status of their application (the system is not easily accessible and updated with the latest information!).
- **Organizational Talent Acquisition**. The HR staff is not fully aware of the business direction, so they are unable to effectively understand and plan for the organizational workforce needs.

### *Process Improvement Initiative*

The VP of Human Resource has appointed an HR resource as the project manager to lead an improvement initiative supported by the process practitioners. The project team will use BPTrends Associates' process-level methodology to conduct this process change, repeated in Figure 12.1.

**Figure 12.1 BPM Methodology Framework**

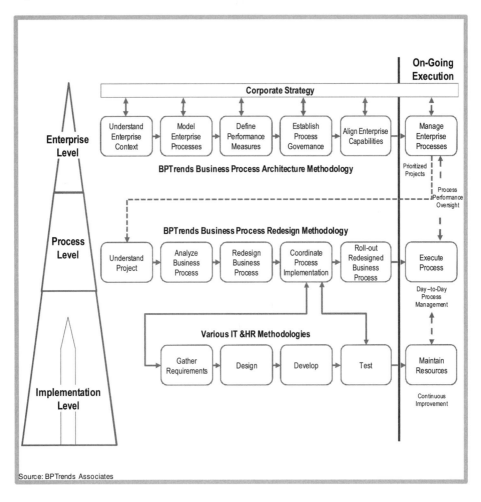

Source: BPTrends Associates

The BPM methodology in Figure 12.1 represents a comprehensive approach to business process management which includes Enterprise-level, Process-level, and Implementation-level activities. In this chapter, my intent is to show the steps as a checklist in the Process-level part of the framework, along with examples of some of the deliverables and templates. The example solutions are for the reader to understand what needs to happen, with some tips on how to utilize some proven techniques. However, this is not a tutorial for the methodology. Note: the checklist steps are a modified version of the BPTrends Associates' Methodology.

## *Methodology Checklist*

In the following checklist, project management steps are clearly distinguished from process management steps. Project Management is an overarching professional practice that drives and oversees process change initiatives. Generally, employees, including analysts and managers, get confused as to what parts belong to which practice. When project delays take place, perhaps due to project management activities, process methodology activities often become the target of finger-pointing as the cause of the delays. The clarity provided by the checklist helps to avoid the blame game of project politics by making all parties understand where the boundaries of these two disciplines intersect.

The purpose of the checklist is to provide an easy way to understand the roadmap of the steps that need to be undertaken for taking a process through the various phases of the methodology. The phases are clearly numbered as 1.0 Understand Project, 2.0 Analyze Business Process, and so on. For clarity, the activities specific to project management versus process management are listed in separate sections of the checklist. While every process initiative may not use all of the steps, the checklist is a way of ensuring that steps are not skipped inadvertently or because of lack of awareness.

### 1.0 UNDERSTAND PROJECT

**Project Management Steps:**

- Develop project description with objectives for process improvement
- Establish project organization and identify process stakeholders
- Provide process orientation and build a collaborative team of stakeholders and analysts
- Identify standards for project execution and deliverables
- Develop and execute plan for Understand Project phase

**Process Management Steps:**

1.1 Plan the project

1.2 Identify process stakeholders; Develop process vision and Key Performance Indicators

1.3 Scope the project for process improvement/redesign

1.4 Develop an initial business case

1.5 Develop plan for human change and stakeholders communication

1.6 Obtain approval to proceed to the Analyze Business Process Phase

**Project Management Steps:**

- Develop detailed project plan
- Initiate business case for change
- Initiate human change plan
- Develop and execute stakeholders communication plan
- Gain approvals

## 2.0 ANALYZE BUSINESS PROCESS

**Process Management Steps:**

2.1 Model and measure as-is process

2.2 Assess as-is process

2.3 Initiate implementation of quick wins

2.4 Plan Redesign Business Process Phase

2.5 Obtain approval to Proceed to the Redesign Business Process Phase

**Project Management Steps:**

- Update business case for change
- Update project plan and coordinate implementation of the quick wins
- Update and execute stakeholders communication plan
- Gain approval
- Assign team members to conduct benchmarks and trends analysis

## 3.0 REDESIGN BUSINESS PROCESS

**Process Management Steps:**

3.1   Develop could-be process design(s)

3.2   Select feasible design

3.3   Finalize to-be process design

3.4   Develop recommendation for implementation

3.5   Develop business case for change

3.6   Obtain approval to proceed to the Coordinate Process Implementation Phase

**Project Management Steps:**

- Finalize business case for change
- Finalize a high-level transformation plan
- Present to management and gain approvals
- Communicate the results to the relevant stakeholders
- Plan for Coordinate Process Implementation Phase

## 4.0 COORDINATE PROCESS IMPLEMENTATION

**Project Management Steps:**

- Plan Implementation Phase
- Delegate development activities to allied groups
- Monitor and coordinate development by allied groups

**Process Management Steps:**

4.1   Create management and measurement systems for redesigned process

4.2   Assemble and test all parts of redesigned process

4.3   Monitor and coordinate development by allied groups

**Project Management Steps:**

- Obtain approval to proceed to Roll-Out Redesigned Business Process Phase

## *How NewAge Foods Completes the Phases*

The HR project manager responsible for the improvement of the Recruit and Hire Employees Process initiates a formal project. He consults with the BPM Business Process Services group (Center of Excellence) regarding methodology and facilitation support; gets direction from the sponsor; obtains commitment from other key stakeholders; forms a team and obtains the necessary resources, including funding and team members' time commitment; and launches the project.

Note: Sometimes the project is initiated and funded only for the Understand Phase to discover the scope of the process, understand the impact of potential changes, and gain a better estimate of cost and time. Each of the phases in the Process-Level methodology is then executed—as appropriate. Every project does not go through every step in the methodology checklist. With their expertise, knowledge, and past experience, guidance from process professionals is essential in deciding the scope of the steps to be covered and the implications of those that would not be done.

In the methodology checklist, both project management and process management steps are listed for completeness. In the details that follow, only process management steps are explored. Except for a few of them, project management steps are out of scope in this book.

### 1.0 UNDERSTAND PROJECT

The outcome of this phase is: an initial description of the problem, a vision of the future state of the process, process and project scope, and a proposal for the scope of the probable analysis and redesign effort for submission to senior management for acceptance and approval to move on to the Analyze Business Process Phase.

### 1.1  *Plan the Project*

The Process Configuration Model in Figure 12.2 may be used as a template to identify project issues, objectives, stakeholders, and other interrelated considerations to create an initial work breakdown structure. The details on this model are outlined in Chapter 7. The project manager would create an initial project plan or a Terms of Reference (initial project intent) at this stage.

**Figure 12.2 Process Configuration Model**

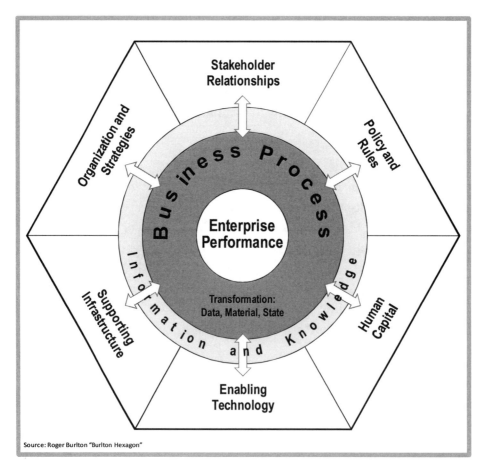

Source: Roger Burlton "Burlton Hexagon"

An initial project plan for conducting the Understand Project Phase is created in this phase. This includes the process goals, project objective, known issues, and opportunities. A project team is assembled from among the process stakeholders who are identified for participation in the analysis and design initiative—and have a vested interest in the performance of the process. Note: all process stakeholders may not necessarily be project stakeholders. While the project has a beginning and an end as a temporary endeavor, the process stakeholders are the perpetual beneficiaries of the process results. This is an initial project plan to understand the project and then develop further details.

### 1.1.1 Understand Process Context

To understand the context and the start and end of the process-in-focus, extract a view from the existing process architecture or blueprint. If architecture does not exist for the Organization-in-Focus, then research existing documents, interview relevant stakeholders, and brainstorm a list of possible steps or sub-processes and show the process workflow in a model format. This deliverable establishes a common understanding among the newly formed team members about the boundaries and initial scope of the process-in-scope. The context diagram becomes a subset of the overall organizational process blueprint. While it is a preliminary cut of a process model, I refer to it as a context diagram so as not to prematurely get into the details of process modeling standards and syntax (however, try to name the processes in verb-noun format).

The process has been detailed into the six sub-processes shown in Figure 12.3. The process begins with sub-process **Identify Needs & Secure Funding**, and ends with **Screen Candidate & Set-up New Employee**. Establishing the boundaries of any process is critical and is the major benefit of creating a context diagram. Later analysis may cause this boundary to be adjusted. As all processes are connected to other processes, the source process that provides inputs to the Process-in-Focus (PIF) and the destination process, where the outputs of the PIF would be received, are identified. These are represented in dotted boxes just to differentiate these external processes from the PIF.

**Figure 12.3 Process Context Diagram**

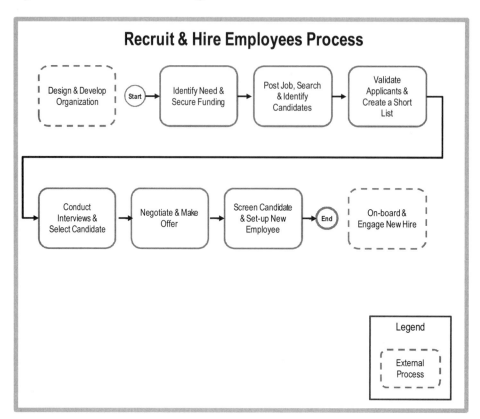

*1.2 Identify Process Stakeholders & Define Process Vision & Key Performance Indicators*

<u>1.2.1 Identify Process Stakeholders for the Selected Process</u>

To formulate the process vision, first list all relevant stakeholders and then identify the key stakeholders. Stakeholders are those individuals or entities who have a vested interest in the success of the process and are the beneficiaries of the process outputs and outcomes. Sometimes even the competition can be a stakeholder. For creating the vision, it is better to identify key stakeholders from among the overall list of stakeholders and create a tentative vision by understanding the key stakeholders' expectations. At a later stage, the vision will be validated by other relevant stakeholders. This approach optimizes the information gathering and development of the vision.

The process stakeholders are identified and a process interaction give-and-get analysis is conducted. Give-and-get is the relationship of the stakeholders with the process. The stakeholders provide something to the process (give) and in return they get something of value back. This relationship is an exchange of value and it must work well for the process to perform at its expected level. The give-and-get relationship provides us with the stakeholders' expectations, from which elements of the process vision can be derived. The value exchanged between the process and the stakeholders become potential KPIs for performance of the process.

In Table 12.1, Stakeholders List, the first column represents the list of stakeholders (can be in any order). The second column is a judgment of which ones are direct versus indirect stakeholders. This is merely a way to get to the third column to narrow down the list of key stakeholders needed for the next step in the analysis. This classification "filter" of direct, indirect, and key may be obvious for some stakeholders, but it may also be a judgment call for others.

**Table 12.1 Process Stakeholders List**

| Stakeholder | Direct/Indirect | Key |
|---|---|---|
| Management | I | |
| Hiring Manager | D | K |
| HR Staff | D | K |
| Candidates (Internal/External) | D | K |
| Recruiters | D | K |

| Stakeholder | Direct/Indirect | Key |
|---|---|---|
| Interview Panel | D | K |
| Payroll/Benefits | I | |
| Facilities | I | |
| IT Services | I | |
| Candidate's Family | I | |
| Compliance Agencies | D | |
| Community | I | |
| Competition | I | |
| Legal | D | K |

In Figure 12.4, Stakeholders Process Interaction, the PIF is in the middle surrounded by the key stakeholders. For each of the stakeholders, the value exchange of what they give to the process and what they get from it is identified. The relationship of this exchange, when measured, would help manage the performance of the process. These are candidates for becoming the Key Performance Indicators in later analysis.

**Figure 12.4 Stakeholders Process Interaction**

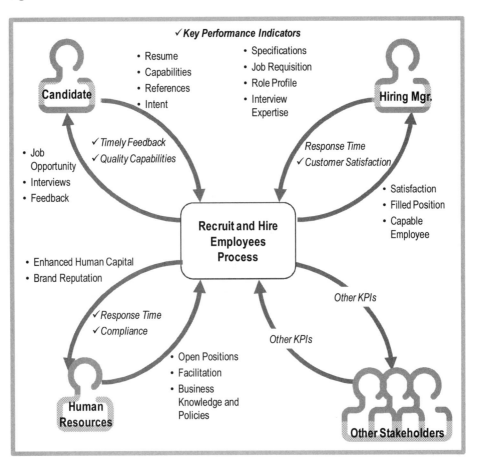

## 1.2.2 Formulate Process Vision & Performance Indicators

The vision describes the stakeholders' perspective of what the process should be in its future state ("begin with end in mind"). For each of the key stakeholders, identify future-state statements that would reflect their expectations. These will be elements of the vision from which a summary statement is derived. The vision elements and the resulting vision statement should be in present tense so as to inspire the feeling that "we have arrived at the desired state". Future tense statements such as "we will be..." continue to state the same words even if you have arrived at the desired state. The vision elements make the vision actionable, in that there are tangible outcomes which can be measured for progress. In some large process change projects, in addition to process vision and vision elements, a slogan or a selling proposition may be created to brand the process and the project. In Figure 12.5, a summarized list of vision elements that is the basis for the process vision statement is shown.

**Figure 12.5 Process Vision**

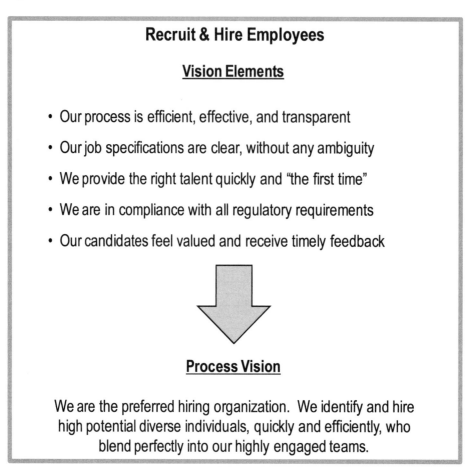

Identify Key Performance Indicators (KPI) for the process-in-focus. The KPI's are a measure by which it is possible to determine if the process is performing and achieving the stated vision. These are the measures of success of the value exchange in the process and stakeholders give-and-get relationship. At this stage, these are known as could-be measures. See Table 12.2.

**Table 12.2 Key Performance Indicators with anticipated target**

| KPI | Vision Target |
|---|---|
| Total Cycle Time (Job requisition to fulfillment) | 4 weeks |
| Wait Time (Candidate response time after decision) | 1 week |
| Key Stakeholders Satisfaction | >98% |
| Process Cost Amount (per candidate) | Reduce by 10% |
| Quality/Competencies of New Hires | >95 percentile of Industry |
| Cost of Non-Conformance | Zero |

## *1.3 Scope the Project for Process Improvement / Redesign*

### 1.3.1 Create a Process Scope Diagram

Gather information using the Inputs, Guides, Outputs, and Enablers (IGOE) method. First identify the process event triggers, and then the outputs. Identification of the outputs helps ensure that the inputs needed are not over-specified. This scope represents a macro-level view of the process. Outputs are the end outcomes of the process. Inputs are those items that are consumed or transformed by the process. The guides are the references that govern/control the process activities and include policies, practices, and knowledge. And the enablers are the reusable resources that include organizational roles, technology (data, systems, and mechanisms), and infrastructure, such as facilities, hardware, and utilities.

An existing Process Architecture/Blueprint is most useful here for identifying process touch points both on input and output of the process-in-scope. This helps eliminate redundancy in the organization and promotes the integrity of the process architecture. If there is no architecture, then this scope diagram can serve as a "bottom up" segment of a future architecture.

The details of the structure of the process scope diagram in Figure 12.6 are outlined in Chapter 4.

**Figure 12.6 Process Scope Diagram**

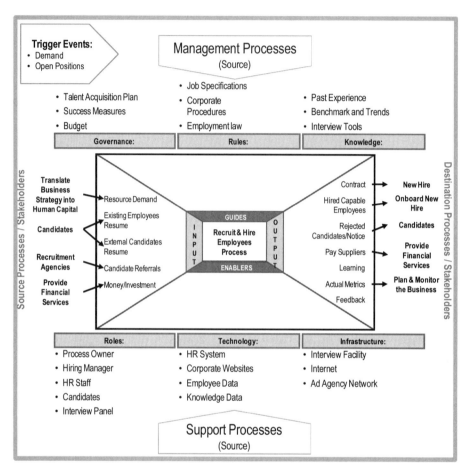

### 1.3.2 Conduct Process Health Check & Establish Scope

Gather information about the problems on all aspects of the scope diagram - Inputs, Guides, Outputs, and Enablers. This is typically done for the current state (as-is), however information is also recorded for known/planned opportunities, such as implementation of a new system. Therefore, at this stage, the Process Scope Diagram is a hybrid of as-is and known to-be items. With the project objectives, constraints, and priorities, identify items of IGOE that will be in the scope of the process improvement for the next phases in the methodology. The legend used in Figure 12.7 determines the condition of the objects around the IGOE.

## Process Health Check Analysis

This analysis is a collaborative activity of the team members. Through consensus on the condition of various items around the IGOE, the scope can be outlined for what would be in the scope of the project going forward and what would be excluded. The process scope at this juncture becomes the project scope for process improvement.

**Figure 12.7 Process "Health Check" Diagram**

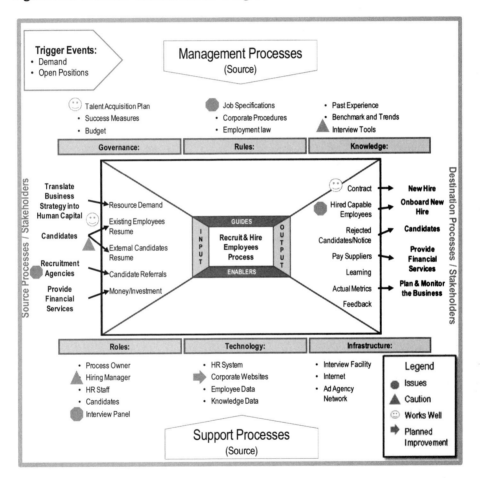

For each input, output, guide, and enabler, gather relevant information for further analysis and development of the initial business case. The issues and opportunities can be classified easily around each of the aspects of IGOE. Figure 12.8 is an example of a template that can be used for information gathering to conduct further impact analysis and identifying actions.

**Figure 12.8 Process Information Gathering and Analysis Template**

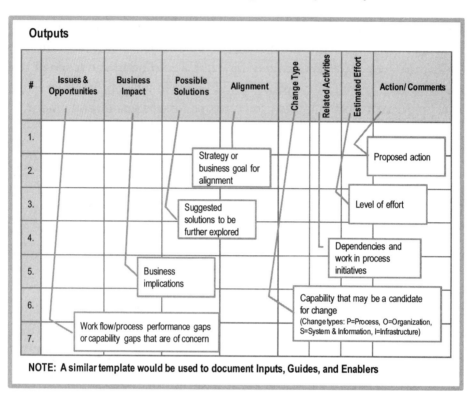

NOTE: A similar template would be used to document Inputs, Guides, and Enablers

## 1.4    Develop an Initial Business Case

Start developing an initial business case driven by the gaps in process performance and the capabilities (organizational roles, technology - systems/data/mechanisms, and infrastructure). This should include the vision elements, KPI's, issues, and opportunities identified in the process scope and the subsequent health check learnings. This initial business case would be updated in Analyze Business Process Phase and then finalized in Redesign Business Process Phase.

## 1.5    Develop Plan for Human Change and Stakeholders Communication

If organizational roles are likely to be impacted, then a plan is needed to address the concerns of the people in those roles by establishing an appropriate policy for human change. Potential organizational design considerations may include changes in roles, jobs, skills, and competencies to optimally align people in support of the changed process. The major concern every employee will have is WIIFM: "What's in it for me?"

### 1.5.1 Determine Human Change Strategy

Human Change Management needs Organization Development and design expertise that uses techniques to assess the impact of change on employees, identifies the best approaches to retooling them for performing on the redesigned process, or helps them explore other options such as reassignment or separation, should some of the employees not accept the changes. One example of a change methodology is the Human Change Transition Curve, shown in Figure 12.9.

**Figure 12.9 The Human Change Transition Curve**

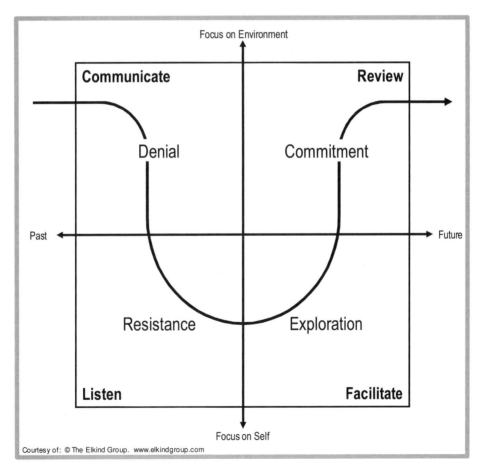

Courtesy of: © The Elkind Group. www.elkindgroup.com

This methodology operates on the theory that people/employees go through four stages of change: Denial, Resistance, Exploration, and Commitment. For a successful change, they must be helped along this curve. There are several versions of this methodology that have been modified for use in a business change context. They are based on the pioneering study of grief and personal trauma by Dr Elisabeth Kubler-Ross.

When in the Denial stage, people want honest communication, which helps them transition into the Resistance stage. There, they want someone in management to listen to and address their concerns. This transitions them into the Exploration stage. Here, employees are helped to explore the possibilities presented by the potential change, such as retooling, relocation, or even honorable separation, in some cases. With effective facilitation, employees will move to the Commitment stage. If not implemented methodically, human changes may not be effective and may result in low morale and productivity.

### 1.5.2 Develop Communication Plan

From the list of process stakeholders, identify groups to whom communication about the status of the project and possible impacts to the process must be directed. The communication plan includes the message, mechanisms, and frequency of delivery, schedule, and assigned responsibility. One of the key elements in this communication would be the inclusion of the Human Change Strategy from Step 1.5.1.

**Table 12.3 Stakeholders Communication Plan**

| Stakeholder Group | Message | Method | Frequency | Who | When | Status |
|---|---|---|---|---|---|---|
| Management | Project Status/Process Scope | In-Person | Quarterly | Process Owner/Project Manager | 30 March | Complete |
| Recruiters | Change in Supplier Agreement | E-Mail and In-person | As Needed | Project Manager & Buying Function | End of Q2 | In Progress |
| Hiring Managers | Process Scope/Issues & Opportunities | E-Mail; Divisional Meetings | As Needed | Process Owner/Project Manager | Beginning of Q2 | Planned |
| Employees | TBD | TBD | TBD | Management? | TBD | TBD |

### 1.6 Obtain Approval to Proceed to the Analyze Business Process Phase

To complete this phase, update the initial project plan with the additional understandings, learnings, and knowledge of the process scope and present the findings of this phase to the project/process sponsor and relevant key stakeholders. Gain their approval to proceed to the next phase, Plan for the Analyze Business Process Phase. Assign responsibilities for the activities needed prior to beginning the next phase.

## 2.0 ANALYZE BUSINESS PROCESS

The outcome of this phase is an analysis of the current state of the process and root cause analysis to clearly understand the nature of the process issues and gaps in performance that must be addressed in the Redesign Phase. The team may pass from this phase to the next without formal approval from the project sponsor or champion.

### 2.1 Model & Measure As-Is Process

#### 2.1.1 Confirm Project Approach & Standards

Reconfirm the project approach for process improvement; establish/confirm process modeling and documentation standards, such as process naming/numbering and the use of agreed-upon documentation tools. This also includes the identification of process improvement analysis tools, such as Reengineering, Lean Six Sigma, or any process simulation tools.

#### 2.1.2 Model Existing Process

If the Process-in-Scope is a high-level process, determine the need to further decompose it into its sub-processes before creating a process flow diagram (swimlane diagram) or a linear flow diagram. For selected sub-processes, a scoping diagram (IGOE) may be needed, as well. When the As-Is state of the process is well understood, there is no need for further exhaustive analysis. I use a Japanese term, "Toriaezu", meaning "it's OK for now", for building consensus among the participants to wrap-up and move on to the next step. Figure 12.10 is a process flow diagram for the PIF. The convention of Swimlanes has been outlined in Figure 6.6 in Chapter 6.

**Figure 12.10 Process Flow Diagram (Note: circles with letters are flow connectors)**

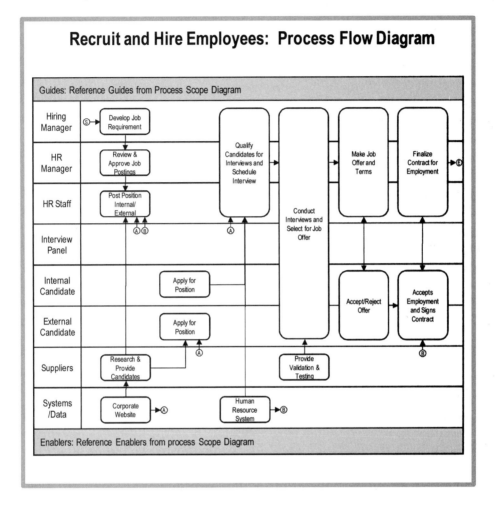

## 2.2   Assess As-is Process

### 2.2.1 Measure Process Performance

Identify a list of Key Performance Indicators and determine the gaps in process performance by comparing them to the desired measures identified in the vision specified in the Understand Project Phase (Reference Step 1.2.2). The KPI Guide in Figure 12.11 helps identify types of performance measures. This is not an exhaustive list, but has only sample KPI's. These KPI's must be aligned with the overall organizational measures.

**Figure 12.11 Key Performance Indicators Guide**

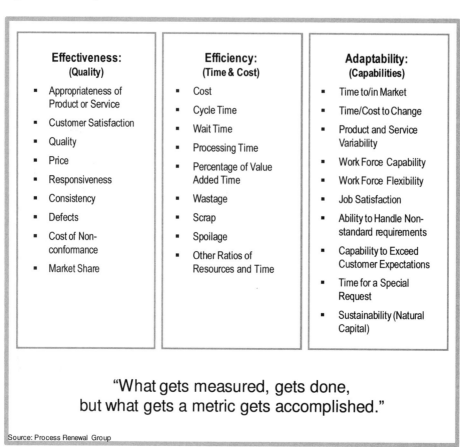

| Effectiveness: (Quality) | Efficiency: (Time & Cost) | Adaptability: (Capabilities) |
|---|---|---|
| ▪ Appropriateness of Product or Service | ▪ Cost | ▪ Time to/in Market |
| ▪ Customer Satisfaction | ▪ Cycle Time | ▪ Time/Cost to Change |
| ▪ Quality | ▪ Wait Time | ▪ Product and Service Variability |
| ▪ Price | ▪ Processing Time | ▪ Work Force Capability |
| ▪ Responsiveness | ▪ Percentage of Value Added Time | ▪ Work Force Flexibility |
| ▪ Consistency | ▪ Wastage | ▪ Job Satisfaction |
| ▪ Defects | ▪ Scrap | ▪ Ability to Handle Non-standard requirements |
| ▪ Cost of Non-conformance | ▪ Spoilage | ▪ Capability to Exceed Customer Expectations |
| ▪ Market Share | ▪ Other Ratios of Resources and Time | ▪ Time for a Special Request |
| | | ▪ Sustainability (Natural Capital) |

"What gets measured, gets done,
but what gets a metric gets accomplished."

Source: Process Renewal Group

Table 12.4 is the result of an analysis to determine current measures and potential future measures. The gaps are identified to then prioritize the measures in terms of importance for planning the implementation in the Redesign Business Process Phase.

**Table 12.4 KPI Performance Analysis**

| Measures Classification | Performance Measure | Strategic Objective/ Stakeholder | Current Measure (As-Is) | Target Measure (To-Be) | Performance Gap | Priority & Plan |
|---|---|---|---|---|---|---|
| Effectiveness (Quality) | New Hire Competencies | Human Capital Strategy | >75 Percentile | >95 Percentile | - 20 Percentile | High |
| | Stakeholders Satisfaction | Internal Processes Scorecard | 80% | 98% | -18% | Medium |
| Efficiency (Time and Cost) | Process Cost Per Candidate | Cost Containment Strategy | $5,000 Per Employee | $4,500 Per Employee | -10% | Medium |
| | Total Cycle Time | Corporate Reputation & Efficient Deployment | 8 Weeks | 4 Weeks | - 4 Weeks | High |
| Adaptability (Capabilities) | Cost of Non Conformance | Zero Tolerance | $500,000 | Zero | -100% | High |
| | Human Capital | TBD | TBD | TBD | TBD | TBD |

### 2.2.2 Analyze the Process

Conduct root cause analysis to identify issues and opportunities using process analysis methods such as Reengineering, Lean, and Six Sigma, as appropriate. The objective is to identify problems that inhibit the desired performance of the process.

**Figure 12.12 Lean Six Sigma Guide: 8 Types of Waste**

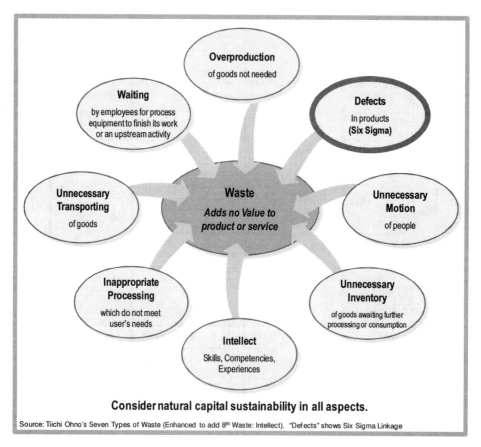

Source: Tiichi Ohno's Seven Types of Waste (Enhanced to add 8th Waste: Intellect). "Defects" shows Six Sigma Linkage

The descriptions of the waste are in terms of the origin of Lean, which was based on materials movement in factories. However, the same concepts are equally applicable to business processes. Originally, there were seven types of waste. An eighth waste has been added - Waste of Intellect. This means not leveraging the skills, competencies, experiences, and ideas of the workforce. The waste type "Defects" is where the Six Sigma tool may be applied. Therefore, in the industry, there is a trend to reference the discipline as Lean Six Sigma. Note that in some organizations, the term used for Lean

Six Sigma is "Turbo Six Sigma", while in others it is "Lean Plus". The name tends to depend on which tool was introduced first in the organization. In Figure 12.12, the "Defects" waste is highlighted to emphasize that here is the Lean and Six Sigma complimentary linkage and thus the concept of Lean Six Sigma is unified.

Additional considerations when analyzing the process include:

- **Sustainability of natural resources.** Also known as natural capital, should be proactively considered when analyzing various types of waste. James Martin, one of the pioneers in Information Technology, recently introduced a new type of measure: *Resource Productivity*. This is concerned with the amount of wealth produced from one unit of natural resources. Business Organizations and Governments are now actively engaged in natural resources conservation initiatives, so in the future, we are likely to see more measures in the area of economic, environmental, and social considerations around sustainability.
- **KPI Gaps and Analysis Tools**. The Key Performance Indicators Guide shown in Figure 12.11 provides an indication of what analysis techniques or tools may be appropriate for which performance gap. Effectiveness and Quality gaps are candidates for Six Sigma usage (Customer Satisfaction, Quality, and so on); Efficiency, Time, and Cost are candidates for the use of Lean (Cycle Time, Waste, and so on); and Adaptability and Capabilities (Product & Service Variability, Workforce Flexibility, and so on) may be candidates for Redesign and Reengineering. While this is by no means an absolute recommendation, it is a consideration for project managers and analysts to think about when planning their process redesign tools approach.

### 2.2.3 Identify & Prioritize Improvement Opportunities

Quick Wins, those that require little effort and cost but provide a desired business benefit for the short term, are identified along with other potential solutions. Opportunities for the Redesign Business Process Phase are documented. Quick Wins identification criteria need to be developed first (Table 12.4), followed by root cause analysis. One of the methods helpful in root cause analysis is the "Fishbone" or Ishikawa technique. It is shown in Figure 12.13 for the **Recruit and Hire Employees** process issue of not getting quality candidates from third party suppliers. Prior to this analysis, the project team would establish the criteria for what qualifies as a Quick Win.

**Table 12.4 Quick Wins Identification Guide (Fishbone or Ishikawa technique)[2]**

| Idea | Redesign | Quick Win |
|---|---|---|
| Number of Organizational Units Impacted | Many | Few |
| Time to Implement | Long | Short |
| Budget Available | Possibly | Certainly |
| Enablers Affected | Many/Heavy | Few/Light |
| Risk | Higher | Low |
| Expected Management Support | Lower | High |
| Expected Staff Resistance | Significant | Little |
| Source of Idea | Team | Worker |

---

[2] Source: Process Renewal Group

In Figure 12.13, Root Cause Analysis, the issue to be analyzed is on the right—"the head of the fish", and the "bones", or branches, are clusters of solution ideas identified through brainstorming. Using the quick wins criteria, items for immediate implementation are identified.

**Figure 12.13 Root Cause Analysis**

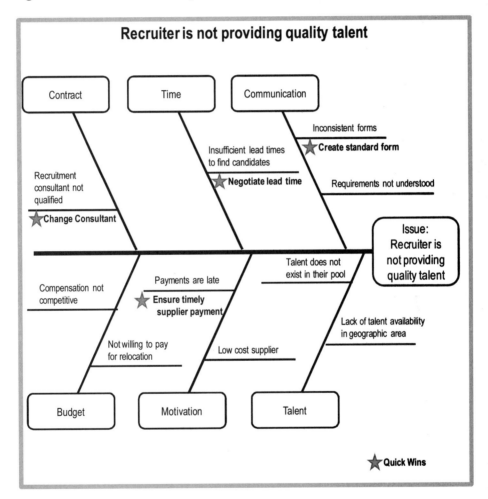

### 2.3 Initiate Implementation of Quick Wins

Develop an implementation plan and assign team responsibilities to implement the agreed on solution. Sometimes quick win solutions are interim solutions only until the To-Be design is implemented. See Table 12.5.

**Table 12.5 Recruiter Issue: Quick Wins Implementation Plan**

| Quick Wins | Implementation Time Frame | Responsible Project Lead |
|---|---|---|
| Develop standard template for job specifications and communicate to all relevant stakeholders (provide job-aids for assistance in the use of the new template) | First Quarter, Year | Name 1 |
| Negotiate and agree on optimized lead times for candidate search with managers and suppliers (review contract and service levels) | First Quarter, Year | Name 2 |

### 2.4 Plan Redesign Business Process Phase

Update the project plan with the pre-work steps needed for the Redesign Business Process Phase, and assign responsibilities to carry out the steps and provide the input for the analysis to be conducted in the next phase. Example: Conduct Benchmark and Trends study for innovative ideas to be considered in process redesign ideation.

### 2.5 Obtain Approval to Proceed to the Redesign Business Process Phase

Update the project plan based on the learnings from the current state analysis. Present the findings from this phase to the project/process sponsor and relevant key stakeholders. Gain approval to proceed to the next phase.

## 3.0 REDESIGN BUSINESS PROCESS

The outcome of this phase is a formal proposal and business case for redesign of the business process, along with a high-level implementation plan for the To-Be process, all submitted to the key stakeholders and senior management for approval.

### 3.1 Develop Could-Be Process Design(s)

#### 3.1.1 Research Innovative Ideas

Research and benchmark processes, trends, and innovative ideas that would include processes and their potential enablers such as organization, technology, and infrastructure using the template in Table 12.6. Based on this research, develop insights that may be used in the process redesign ideation to create one or multiple could-be design possibilities.

**Table 12.6 Process Redesign Research and Information Gathering**

| Business Change | Benchmarks | Trends | Innovation |
|---|---|---|---|
| Process: products, services, and ways of working... | | Shared services for HR Recruitment | Possible co-sharing of Recruitment services with other businesses |
| Guides: governance, rules, and knowledge... | University recruitment fairs | Reward current employees to help attract proven talent | |

| Business Change | Benchmarks | Trends | Innovation |
|---|---|---|---|
| Enablers: human capital; organization design, workforce capabilities... | | Demographics: Generation X, Y work preferences | Hire Generation X and Y employees as hiring staff |
| Enablers: technology, application systems, data, and information... | | Social media is a tool for business communication | Integrate social media network to seek candidates |
| Enablers: infrastructure, facilities, utilities, communication technical platforms... | | | Provide high-tech work stations for employees |

Insights: The workforce demographics are changing with generations X, Y, and Millennials, in the workforce. To attract and retain employees of this generation, the Recruit and Hire Employees Process must accommodate social media as one of the sources of recruitment. Work compensation and support practices must be enhanced to attract and retain competent talent.

### 3.1.2 Establish Evaluation Criteria

Based on the understanding gained from previous phases and your research, identify the criteria that will be used to select the new design. The criteria is deduced from a synthesis of the project objectives outlined by management, the process vision, performance gaps, opportunities, and any unique ideas that would give a competitive edge to the process performance. Using suitable brainstorming techniques, gain consensus among the stakeholders for how the new design will be judged for viability in the organization. See the example in Figure 12.14.

**Figure 12.14 Process Redesign Criteria**

- Customer influenced outcomes (versus outputs)
- Clear process value proposition and performance measures
- Clear expectations, accountability, and motivation— with measures
- The right information to the right people at the right time for the right reasons
- Single source of information and tools (pull versus push)
- Eliminate all waste: Minimize exceptions (standardize the process); eliminate over specification of requirements (do not compromise innovation steps)
- Consider promoting sustainability wherever possible (natural capital)

### *3.2    Select Feasible Design*

#### 3.2.1 Formulate Alternatives & Model Potential Solutions

Explore unconstrained alternative solutions for the opportunities identified in the previous phases and research new ideas. Identify could-be process design solutions ranging from potential solutions based on a pure vision of the process to that of lesser scope. This is the step where innovation and outside-the-box thinking are essential for developing new and improved solutions. The O'Reilley-Tusman model in Figure 12.15 shows the range of innovations possible in various dimensions of change.

**Figure 12.15 Process Innovation Guide**

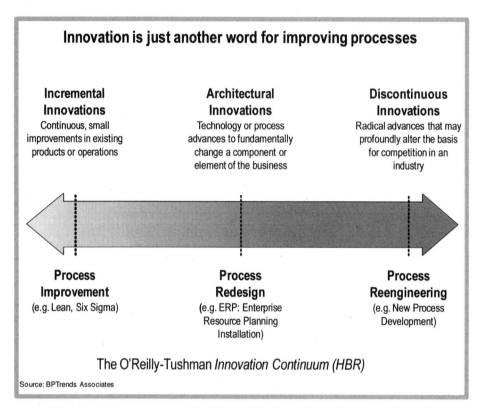

The O'Reilly-Tushman *Innovation Continuum (HBR)*

Source: BPTrends Associates

There are numerous approaches, methods, and tools for developing ideas that can be utilized for improvements and innovation. What you use is dependent on your organizational culture, the makeup of the project team and process stakeholders, and the capability for conducting ideation. In general, ideation methods are out of scope of this book. However, a couple of useful methods are introduced in Figures 12.16, Lotus Blossom, and 12.17, Town Hall Ideation.

Ideation methods and tools may be classified into the following categories:

- **Unstructured**. Brainstorming, Brain Writing, and Town Hall Ideation.
- **Semi-Structured**. Brain Sailing and Lotus Blossom.
- **Structured**. TRIZ (and P-TRIZ) (pronounced "trees") is a Romanized acronym for a Russian word "The theory of inventor's problem solving". It was developed by a Soviet

engineer and researcher, Genrich Altshuller, and today it is a methodology, tool set, knowledge base, and model-based technology for generating innovative ideas and solutions for problem solving[3]. Howard Smith has developed a version of TRIZ and P-TRIZ adapted for business process innovation.

- **Biomimicry.** Biomimicry (from *bios*, meaning life, and *mimesis*, meaning to imitate) or learning from nature, is a design discipline that seeks sustainable solutions by emulating nature's time-tested patterns and strategies.

**Figure 12.16 Lotus Blossom Ideation Template**

| | | | | | | | | |
|---|---|---|---|---|---|---|---|---|
| 6 | 3 | 7 | 6 | 3 | 7 | 6 | 3 | 7 |
| 2 | F | 4 | 2 | C | 4 | 2 | G | 4 |
| 5 | 1 | 8 | 5 | 1 | 8 | 5 | 1 | 8 |
| 6 | 3 | 7 | F | C | G | 6 | 3 | 7 |
| 2 | B | 4 | B | Main Idea | D | 2 | D | 4 |
| 5 | 1 | 8 | E | A | H | 5 | 1 | 8 |
| 6 | 3 | 7 | 6 | 3 | 7 | 6 | 3 | 7 |
| 2 | E | 4 | 2 | A | 4 | 2 | H | 4 |
| 5 | 1 | 8 | 5 | 1 | 8 | 5 | 1 | 8 |

Concept Developed by Yasuo Matsumura of Clover Management Research, Chiba City, Japan

---

[3] From Wikipedia

In Lotus Blossom, you start with a problem or area of concern in the center core of the Lotus Blossom template. Ideas for possible solutions are then generated around the core area of concern. Taking one of the emerging themes, create another core and expand upon it. This approach provides many possibilities which can be prioritized based on the ideation criteria and within the limits of given constraints. This method works well in smaller groups for one given problem area at a time. The Town Hall Ideation method in Figure 12.17 is effective with larger groups and entails brainstorming in the various themes of the metaphor of township planning: Heritage Preservation, and Neighborhood Improvement.

**Figure 12.17 "Sabean" Town Hall Ideation**

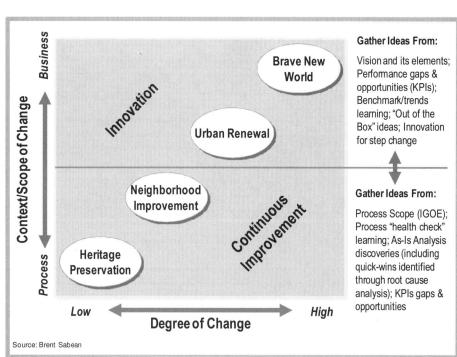

Sub-groups can be assigned different themes to brainstorm for ideas within a certain range, and later given the opportunity to participate in the themes of other groups. Each of the sub-groups is instructed to gather and include information generated in this and previous phases. The ideas generated are further prioritized, as appropriate. General brainstorming guidelines, apply in both Lotus Blossum and Town Hall Ideation. See Table 12.7.

**Table 12.7 Result of Brainstorming**

The identifiers A, B, C, and so on, are only for reference—they do not imply priority or sequence.

| Small Ideas | Reference Identifiers | Big Ideas | Reference Identifiers |
|---|---|---|---|
| Evaluate current recruiting agencies against others available | A | Remove third party recruiters and in-source all recruitment | H |
| Communicate lead times: work back from employee start date | B | Establish effective succession planning for continuous talent pipeline | I |
| Use temporary help in HR to meet demand | C | Create shared services organization for cross-unit recruitment | J |
| Interview for core competencies in pre-screening of candidates | D | Partner with universities to source qualified candidates | K |
| Standardize and automate job description templates | E | Offer relocation to attract better talent | L |
| Expand interview panel pool to ensure timely availability | F | Standardize transition time for internal candidates to fill open positions in a timely manner | M |
| Provide methods and tools to interview panel for effectiveness in selection | G | Offer state of the art benefits befitting the demographics of the current work force | N |

Once the ideas are gathered, they need to be rationalized in terms of the level of effort required and their feasibility. There are a variety of methods that may be used to perform a high-level analysis, including the one in Figure 12.18 that uses a Payoff Matrix. On one axis is the impact of changes and on the other, the ease of implementation. Multiple could-be scenarios are created from the result of the ideation to ensure all possible options are evaluated. The following classification provides the scope of further analysis and investigation.

The items in quadrants 1 to 4 are high priority candidates that would provide significant benefit with easy to moderate effort; items in quadrants 5 to 8 require further evaluation, and items in quadrant 9 would not be desirable solutions. The example uses the reference letters in the previous figure.

**Figure 12.18 Payoff Matrix**

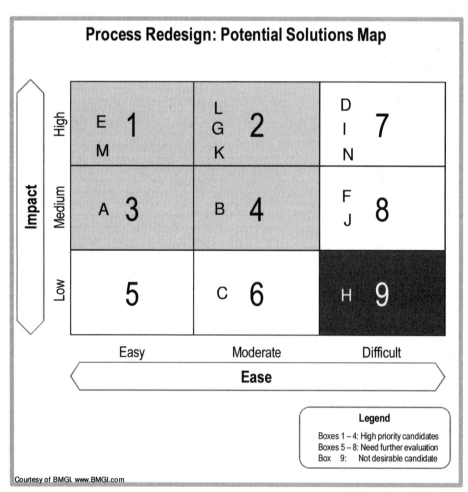

### 3.3    *Finalize To-Be Process Design*

Understand project constraints and further prioritize opportunities for the various possible solutions. Create one To-be design from the multiple Could-be options. Identify fundamental data entities and develop a process conceptual data model. This model provides a high-level understanding of the data needs and will be the basis for data and business rules development. Validate the design for viability using the process event triggers for scenarios, prototyping, and so on. The project team should demonstrate to management that effort has been made to develop unique solutions for giving the organization a competitive edge. Figure 12.19 contains examples of questions to be addressed by the project team. Deliverable examples of this step are: the to-be process flow in diagram Figure 12.20; fundamental data entities in Table 12.8; and the process conceptual data model in Figure 12.21.

**Figure 12.19 Questions of Excellence**

- What is unique in the solution that will enhance the capability of the Process / Organization / Technology / Infrastructure?

- What will provide a sustainable competitive advantage?

- What is it that would provide customer delight (value+)?

- What idea/solution will promote sustainability of Natural Capital?

  "The difference between Ordinary and Extraordinary is the word EXTRA."

**Figure 12.20 To-Be Design Process Flow Diagram**

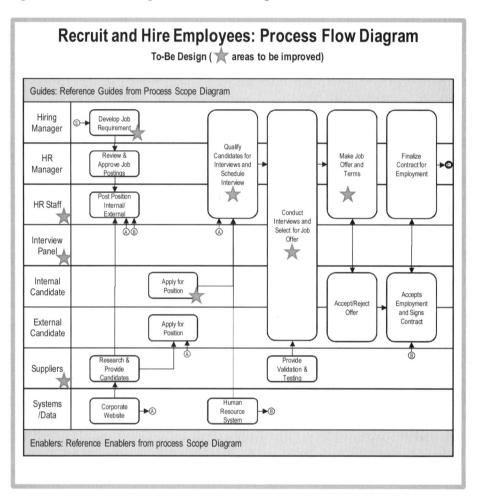

These data entities are used to construct the conceptual data model. See Table 12.8.

**Table 12.8 Fundamental Data Entities**

| Data Entities for Process-in-Scope |
|---|
| Competency (Development, Learning Solution) |
| Location (Country) |
| Organizational Entity (Legal, Business Unit, Cost Center) |
| Person (Employee, Candidate) |
| Person: Employee (Qualification, Language) |
| Position (Post, Grade, Function) |
| Time |

Figure 12.21 is the conceptual data model for PIF. There is a possibility that for a subset of the model, a more detailed logical data model would have to be developed. The concepts of data models are detailed in Chapter 6.

Figure 12.21 Process Conceptual Data Model for To-Be Design

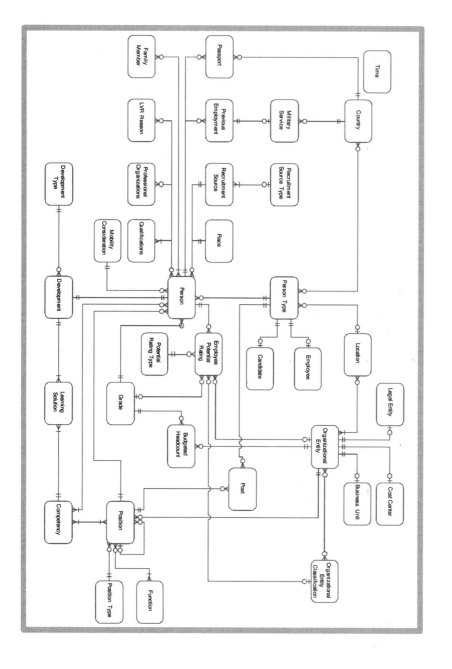

### *3.4    Develop Recommendation for Implementation*

With an understanding of the project constraints, prioritize design options based on potential opportunities, project objectives, and constraints. Develop a recommendation for implementation that can be incorporated into the business case for change. The Gap Model in Figure 12.22 describes the basic elements that must be addressed in the business case for change.

**Figure 12.22 Performance Gap Analysis Model**

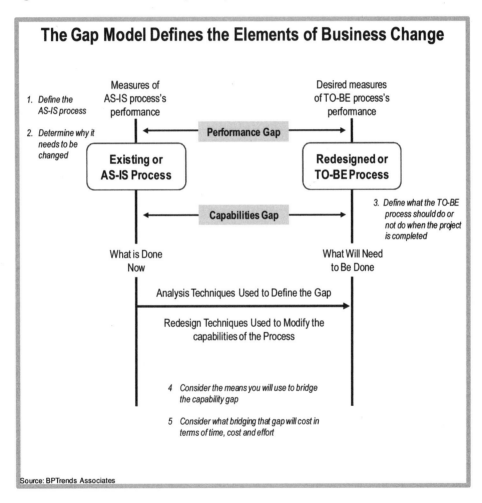

The starting point for business change is the gap in performance and capabilities--what the gap is and what should be done to close it. The objective should be to exceed the performance and capabilities objectives through step changes and innovation, where possible. The capabilities would include processes, organization, technology, systems, data, and infrastructure.

Process change includes changes to the enablers and possibly changes to the upstream and downstream processes. Therefore, a process change program that includes interrelated projects needs to be identified and coordinated with PMO.

For communication and justification to management and key stakeholders, a comparison such as the one in Table 12.9, is very useful.

**Table 12.9 Process Change Benefits: Proposed Transformation from As-Is to the To-Be Design**

| As-Is Process | Transformation Parameters | To-Be Process |
|---|---|---|
| HR generalist staff specializes in job types for hiring employees | Increased workforce capability; Reduction of cycle time | HR Staff will be cross-trained to handle multiple specializations |
| Recruiter capability lacks competitive offering of talent | High caliber talent sourcing in a timely manner | Best in class recruiters will be selected with clear service level agreements |
| Recruitment and Hiring information is not integrated and is largely manual | Consistent and single sourcing of synthesized data; integrity in reporting | Recruitment and Hiring information will be integrated and automated |

### 3.5 Develop Business Case for Change

Finalize the business case that justifies the return on investment and develop a high-level implementation plan. The business case should include the As-Is process, gaps in performance and capabilities, and rationale for recommending the To-Be solution. The implementation plan should include changes to processes, organization, and technology infrastructure.

The business case for process change can be defined in a variety of formats, depending on corporate standards and preferences. Here is an outline of a business case template. It contains five building blocks of change justification:

- Strategic Fit
- Options Appraisal
- Commercial Aspects
- Affordability
- Achievability

Each of these areas has relevant topics populated from the deliverables produced throughout the previous phases of the process improvement process.

- **Strategic Fit**. Consider business need, organizational overview, contribution to organizational objectives, stakeholders, scope (minimum, desirable, and optional), constraints, dependencies, strategic and operational benefits, strategic and operational risks, critical success factors to business change.
- **Options Appraisal**. Consider the long and short list of options, opportunities for innovation and collaboration, cost benefit analysis, risk quantification and cost of change, benefits appraisal, implementation options, and summary of the preferred option.
- **Commercial Aspects**. Consider summary of resource requirements, sourcing options, financial allocations, contractual requirements, human resource issues, and high-level view of implementation timescale.
- **Affordability**. Consider budget based on whole life cost of change, including impacts to upstream and downstream processes, procurement strategy, income and expenditure account.
- **Achievability**. Consider similar projects' success information, assumptions outline, industry comparisons,

program/project outline and key roles, transformation plan, contract management, risk management strategy, benefits realization plan, project evaluation reviews, post implementation review, and contingency plan.

### 3.6 Obtain Approval to Proceed to the Coordinate Process Implementation Phase

Update the stakeholders' communication plan, present the business case, and gain approvals to proceed to the next phase. This may result in the initiation of multiple projects, possibly including projects for process, organization, technology, infrastructure. A Project Management Office (PMO) would play an important role in this step and beyond.

### 4.0 COORDINATE PROCESS IMPLEMENTATION

The outcome of this phase is all changes in process management, work assignments, job descriptions, and software applications are complete, have been tested, and are ready to be used in support of the new process. Two sample tools are noteworthy in this phase: Process Configuration Model, which is addressed in Chapter 7, and The Zachman Framework. Process Configuration Model Figure 12.2, which was used earlier in the Understand Project Phase, can be used here again for identifying work streams for implementation and for understanding the various professional practices that are required in the implementation phase. The Zachman Framework helps develop enterprise architecture and understand different perspectives of an organization, which can help identify which analysis techniques can be used to describe specific components of the framework. Establish a protocol and transfer redesigned specifications and the business case for change to the allied groups for design and implementation of various guides, enablers, and other relevant considerations.

At this stage, the activities to be initiated include: Business Process Management and Measurement System; Business Functional Requirements Definition; Organization Design; Business Data Models and Definition; Inbound/Outbound Interface Definitions; and Technology Definitions including IT.

### 4.1 Create Management & Measurement Systems for Redesigned Process

The agreed upon and prioritized measures of the redesigned process will be implemented at this stage. Consensus on the measures, their definitions, and KPIs' would be gained; the data needed and its sources would be identified; protocols for the collection of data and its reporting to the process owners will be established.

### 4.2 Assemble & Test All Parts of Redesigned Process

All parts, including inputs, outputs, guides, and enablers, should be tested for their new, streamlined operation. This includes the inputs and outputs to the interdependent processes and stakeholders. Also, develop training materials and a communication to all stakeholders for a readiness check.

### 4.2 Monitor & Coordinate Development by Allied Groups

Each allied group has its professional methodologies which are initiated to define, design, develop, test, and implement solutions for their respective areas. Prior to the kick off, each of these professional areas should develop their individual business cases for change and gain appropriate resources. The business cases are driven by the overall business case for change for the new process(es).

### 5.0 ROLL-OUT REDESIGNED BUSINESS PROCESS

The outcome of this phase **is** the new process which is now the norm:

- The process redesign team no longer involved with process (the team would conduct an after action review for capturing learnings and may plan for a post implementation review, allowing some time for process operation to settle down. The project manager thanks all stakeholders for the success and archives project artifacts.
- The day-to-day process manager has to ensure the performance of the new process. In order to do so, the day-to-day manager would be trained in the collection, analysis, and reporting of metrics.
- Look for additional opportunities to improve the process. Based on the after action review, the project manager would

document ideas for further improvements to the process and hand that over to the process manager for inclusion in the next cycle of process change.

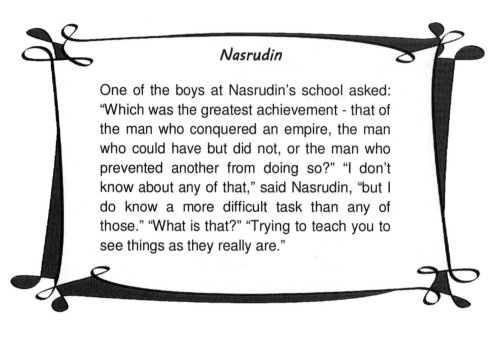

### Nasrudin

One of the boys at Nasrudin's school asked: "Which was the greatest achievement - that of the man who conquered an empire, the man who could have but did not, or the man who prevented another from doing so?" "I don't know about any of that," said Nasrudin, "but I do know a more difficult task than any of those." "What is that?" "Trying to teach you to see things as they really are."

Such is the journey of "How Work Gets Done." Good luck.

**American Productivity & Quality Center (APQC).** "Process Classification Framework (PCF) Cross-Industry" can be downloaded free from www.apqc.org/pcf.

**BPM Methodology** is sourced from: Paul Harmon and Business Process Trends. *Business Process Change, Second Edition, A Guide for Business Managers and BPM and Six Sigma Professionals.* Burlington, MA, Morgan Kaufman Publishers, 2007. (Refer to chapters 8 and 12).

**Business Case Template** used in Chapter 12 is sourced from the Office of Government Commerce (OGC), HM Treasury, UK. See www.ogc.gov.uk/documents/BusinessCaseTemplate-DetailedContent.doc.pdf.

**Business Functions & Processes** concept used in Chapter 1 is sourced from: Rummler, Geary A., and Brache, Alan P. *Improving Performance: How to Manage the White Space in the Organization Chart.* San Francisco, CA: Jossey-Bass Inc., 1995.

**Business Process Modeling Notation (BPMN)** is a standard to model Business Process flows, created by the Business Process Management Initiative (BPMI) and now managed by the Object Management Group (OMG). Visit www.BPMI.org and www.OMG.org. For easy to understand usage examples, see www.bpmn-introduction.com and www.bpmn-introduction.com/HumanReadableBPMNDiagrams.pdf.

**Learning Framework 70/20/10** was developed by Morgan McCall, Robert W. Eichinger, and Michael M. Lombardo at the Center for Creative Leadership www.ccl.org. An overview is available at: http://www.princeton.edu/hr/learning/philosophy.

**Nasrudin Stories** are sourced from: Shah, Idries: *The Exploits of the Incredible Mulla Nasrudin* and *The Subtleties of the Inimitable Mulla Nasrudin.* London, England: Octagon Press, Limited, 1983. *The Pleasantries of the Incredible Mulla Nasrudin.* New York, NY: Arkana Books, 1993.

**Process Configuration Model,** a.k.a Burlton Hexagon, is a concept developed by Roger Burlton. However, the name Process Configuration Model is assigned to this tool by Arjit Mahal and Alexandre Magno Mello. For the original concept, see Chapter 5 in *Business Process Management: Profiting from Process* by Roger T. Burlton, Sam's Publishing, 2001.

**Process Scope Diagram IGOE** process modeling notation had originated as a part of the IDEF, a standard in the modeling language funded by the US Air Force and used in the Department of Defense. Later, Roger Burlton modified the terms 'constraint/control' to guides and 'resources' to enablers in the process model, thus now being referred to as the Burlton Model. See Chapter 12 in *Business Process Management: Profiting from Process* by Roger T. Burlton, Sam's Publishing, 2001.

**Software Tools** Chapter 11 is taken from BPTrends' report on the state of software tools: Wolf, Celia, and Harmon, Paul. "The State of Business Process Management, 2010." Business Process Trends. See *www.bptrends.com/surveys_landing.cfm.*

**The Zachman Framework™** is the fundamental structure for Enterprise Architecture and thereby yields the total set of descriptive representations relevant for describing an Enterprise. See *www.zachmanframeworkassociates.com.*

**Town-Hall Ideation** technique, referred to in Chapter 12, was developed by Brent Sabean, and then enhanced by Arjit Mahal to include sources for gathering process information.

**Transition Curve** used in Chapter 12 is used with the permission of The Elkind Group. www.elkindgroup.com. This and various other models used in the human change are based on the original study on grief by Dr Elisabeth Kübler-Ross who pioneered methods in the support and counseling of personal trauma, grief and grieving, associated with death and dying. See www.businessballs.com/elisabeth_kubler_ross_five_stages_of_grief.htm.

**TRIZ** Chapter 12: (pronounced "trees"), is a Romanized acronym for a Russian word "The theory of inventor's problem solving". It was developed by a Soviet engineer and researcher, Genrich Altshuller, and today, it is a methodology, tool set, knowledge base, and model-based technology for generating innovative ideas and solutions for problem solving. Howard Smith has developed a version of TRIZ, P-TRIZ, that is adapted for business process innovation. See *wikipedia.org/wiki/TRIZ.*

**Value Proposition** concept in Chapter 10 is referenced from: Treacy, Michael, and Wiersema, Fred. *The Discipline of Market Leaders.* New York, NY: HarperCollins Publishers, 1995. The diagram is created by Artie Mahal.

| | |
|---|---|
| **5 Why's** | Drilling down to the root cause of a problem |
| **70/20/10** | Learning (Development) Framework |
| **APQC** | American Productivity & Quality Center |
| **BAM** | Business Activity Monitoring |
| **BI** | Business Intelligence |
| **BPA** | Business Process Architecture |
| **BPDM** | Business Process Definition Metamodel |
| **BPEL** | Business Process Execution Language |
| **BPM** | Business Process Management |
| **BPMM** | Business Process Maturity Model |
| **BPMN** | Business Process Modeling Notation |
| **BPMS** | Business Process Management System |
| **BPO** | Business Process Owner |
| **BPS** | Business Process Services |
| **CDM** | Conceptual Data Model |
| **CEO** | Chief Executive Officer |
| **CIO** | Chief Information Officer |

| | |
|---|---|
| **CMMI** | Capability Maturity Model for Integration |
| **CPI** | Continuous Process Improvement |
| **CPO** | Chief Process Officer |
| **DMAIC** | Define, Measure, Analyze, Improve, Control |
| **EA** | Enterprise Architecture |
| **EAI** | Enterprise Application Integration |
| **ER Diagram** | Entity Relationship Diagram |
| **ERP** | Enterprise Resource Planning |
| **IGOE** | Input, Guides, Output, Enablers |
| **IT** | Information Technology |
| **KPI** | Key Performance Indictor |
| **LDM** | Logical Data Model |
| **OD** | Organization Development/Design |
| **OIF** | Organization-in-Focus |
| **PCM** | Process Configuration Model |
| **PDM** | Physical Data Model |
| **PIF** | Process-in-Focus |
| **PMO** | Program Management Office |
| **P-TRIZ** | Modified version of TRIZ |

| | |
|---|---|
| **QA** | Quality Assurance |
| **QC** | Quality Control |
| **ROI** | Return on Investment |
| **SAM** | Subject Area Model |
| **SCAMPER** | Substitute, Combine, Adapt, Modify/Magnify, Put to other use, Eliminate/Minimize, Reverse/Rearrange |
| **SDLC** | Systems Development Life Cycle |
| **SIPOC** | Supplier, Input, Process, Output, Customer |
| **SME** | Subject Matter Expert |
| **SOA** | Service-Oriented Architecture |
| **SOP** | Standard Operating Procedure |
| **SWOT** | Strengths, Weaknesses, Opportunities, and Threats |
| **TORIAEZU** | Japanese phrase "It's OK For Now" (pronounced Tori-ia-zoo) |
| **TQM** | Total Quality Management |
| **TRIZ** | Russian acronym for "Theory of Inventive Problem Solving" usually pronounced "trees" |
| **VOB** | Voice of the Business |
| **VOC** | Voice of the Customer |

| | |
|---|---|
| **VOP** | Voice of Process |
| **WBS** | Work Breakdown Structure |
| **XML** | Extensible Markup Language |